LESS HYPE, MORE HELP:

Reducing Juvenile Crime, What Works -- and What Doesn't

Richard A. Mendel

American Youth Policy Forum
Child Welfare League of America
Coalition for Juvenile Justice
National Collaboration for Youth
National Crime Prevention Council
National League of Cities, Institute for Youth, Education, and Families
National Urban League

CO-PUBLISHERS' NOTE

The co-publishers of the report join together to present the valuable perspectives on juvenile crime of the report's author, Richard A. Mendel. Our common goal is to foster a more reasoned national discussion about the complex and very important challenges posed by youth crime in America, and to raise public awareness about promising approaches to youth crime that currently receive too little attention and too few resources. The co-publishers do not subscribe to every conclusion and recommendation in the document, but we are unanimous in our view that the issues raised here merit serious attention throughout the nation.

ABOUT THE AUTHOR

Richard Mendel is an independent writer, researcher and consultant on poverty-related issues in youth development, neighborhood safety, employment and training, and community economic development. He worked for four years at South Bronx Overall Economic Development Corporation, ending in 1998 as Assistant Vice President for Program Development and Evaluation. From 1986 to 1991 he worked as a staff associate for MDC, Inc., a non-profit employment policy research firm in Chapel Hill, N.C. In addition, Mr. Mendel has completed projects for the Enterprise Foundation, Wallace-Reader's Digest Fund, Lilly Endowment, Corporation for Enterprise Development, and Surdna Foundation, among others. Mr. Mendel has written for *The Atlantic, Washington Post, Miami Herald, Baltimore Sun, Washington Monthly,* and others. Previously, for the American Youth Policy Forum, Mr. Mendel wrote *The American School-to-Career Movement: A Background Paper for Policy Makers and Foundation Officers* (1994), and *Prevention or Pork: A Hard-Headed Look at Youth-Oriented Anti-Crime Programs* (1995). Mr. Mendel holds a bachelor's degree in public public policy from Duke University (1983) and a master's in journalism from the University of Maryland (1992).

Editors at the American Youth Policy Forum include Samuel Halperin, Betsy Brand, Glenda Partee, Donna Walker James and Steve Estes. Sarah Pearson designed the covers. Rafael Chargel formatted the document for publication. Substantive input on the text of the manuscript was provided by Jack Calhoun, Nancy Gannon, Clifford Johnson, Jean O'Neil and Gordon Raley.

CONTENTS

OVERVIEW

America has both the knowledge and the money we need to substantially reduce adolescent crime and youth violence. We have the know-how to reduce the number of young people likely to join the next generation of adult criminals. Better yet, we can likely achieve this goal at a cost no greater (and perhaps considerably less) than what we will spend if current juvenile justice policies and programs remain in place.

That's the good news. The bad news is that – at all levels of government – the changes necessary to win the battle against juvenile crime are not being enacted. Even worse, many local, state and federal leaders have instead been passing laws and funding programs that simply don't work – including some very expensive efforts that may actually increase juvenile crime.

These so-called "reforms" have been implemented with strong public support – propelled by a barrage of sensationalized news coverage in recent years spotlighting heinous crimes committed by young people. Juvenile crime has become front-page news. Public opinion polls have found ever-increasing support for harsher punishment of juvenile offenders. Political leaders across the nation have responded in lock step.

Virtually every state in the nation enacted legislation in the 1990s either mandating the transfer of youthful offenders to adult courts or easing the legal process for prosecutors and judges to do so. Most states have also increased punishments for juvenile offenders and/or included juvenile convictions in adult "three strikes and you're out" laws. Most have scaled back privacy protections that historically shielded the identities of juvenile offenders, and most states and cities have significantly expanded the bed capacity of their juvenile detention centers and locked correctional facilities. The federal government has jumped in as well – requiring states to consider new laws to try more youths in adult court as a condition for receiving federal delinquency prevention and juvenile justice funding.

These changes have been made with hardly a whisper of public opposition. As criminologist Peter Greenwood of the RAND Corporation has written, "In recent years it has become fashionable for just about every candidate for public office to have a position on crime, and the only position worth having is appearing to be tougher than your opponent."

But do these approaches to juvenile crime work? Do they produce the results we want – lower rates of delinquency, reduced recidivism among youthful offenders – and at a reasonable cost? Do research and experience demonstrate that these are the most successful and cost-effective approaches to combatting adolescent crime? Or have other less-utilized policies and programs proven more effective? Addressing these questions is essential for any successful response to adolescent crime. Yet such questions have been seldom asked in the stampede to "get tough" with delinquent children and youth.

In August 1999, the Walter S. Johnson Foundation asked the American Youth Policy Forum to review the available evidence and answer these important public policy questions. What works in reducing juvenile crime? What doesn't work? What is commonplace today in juvenile justice and crime prevention, and what changes are required to ensure that publicly funded programs are delivered in accordance with best practice?

A nine-month investigation – including visits to juvenile justice and delinquency prevention programs across the country, interviews with dozens of academics and practitioners, and analysis of thousands of pages of public documents, statistics, and scholarly research – led inexorably to the conclusion pronounced above: ***America has the knowledge we need to reduce adolescent crime and violence without a substantial long-term increase in spending. Yet the policy and program reforms necessary to win the battle against juvenile crime are not being enacted.***

This report is divided into three sections. **Part One** details the wealth of new knowledge about the causes and cures for delinquency and youth violence that has been generated by researchers and practitioners over the past two decades, including powerful new models that are dramatically reducing recidivism by youthful offenders and the onset of delinquency by high-risk youth. **Part Two** examines two popular notions that have monopolized the public debate in recent years and prevented policymakers from recognizing the tremendous potential created by the advances in prevention and intervention techniques: that youth crime is growing worse due to a generation of "juvenile superpredators"; and that "adult time for adult crime" should be the basis for juvenile crime policy. **Part Three** looks in detail at our nation's juvenile justice systems and our varied efforts to prevent delinquency and violence. What are we currently doing, and how well does it work? What are the barriers to implementing more effective programs and practices grounded in sound research? Finally, the report issues a series of recommendations – strategic action to surmount the formidable obstacles to reform that now prevent state and local juvenile justice and delinquency prevention systems from doing what works.

Specifically, the report finds:

- **Over the past two decades, prevention and juvenile justice policy innovators have developed and validated a number of intervention models that substantially lower either recidivism by youthful offenders or the onset of delinquent behavior by youth at risk for delinquency.**

For youth who do not pose an immediate threat to public safety, ***most of the winning strategies work with young people in their own homes and communities, rather than in institutions, and they focus heavily on the family environment.*** One strategy, called Multisystemic Therapy, has cut recidivism rates of chronic juvenile offenders by 25 to 70 percent in a series of rigorous clinical trials – and MST costs only $4,500 per youth, less than one-fourth the cost of an eight-month stay in juvenile corrections. Another home-based strategy, Functional Family Therapy, has also reduced the recidivism rates of delinquent youth by 25 to 80 percent in repeated trials. It costs only $2,000 per youth.

Researchers have also produced valuable information on the causes, correlates and developmental pathways leading to delinquency, and they have identified a solid set of core principles to guide effective prevention practice. Meanwhile, juvenile justice reformers have demonstrated many best practices that markedly improve the success of youth in juvenile courts and corrections systems while saving a significant percentage of taxpayer funds now spent on juvenile justice. The experts still have a world of work to do in honing and refining their instruments, but ***the basic tools are now available to substantially improve our nation's juvenile justice and delinquency prevention systems.***

- **Alarmist rhetoric about a new generation of juvenile "superpredators" and a "ticking time bomb" of juvenile crime pervaded the public consciousness during the 1990s and diverted political leaders' attention from the crucial task of investing in what works. This rhetoric was unfounded.**

After a sharp upswing during the late 1980s and early 1990s, juvenile crime and violence have fallen sharply. ***By 1998, the latest year for which data are now available, the juvenile homicide***

rate had declined by 52 percent from its 1993 high – bringing the rate to its lowest level since 1987. The combined rates for all serious violent offenses (murder, rape, robbery, and aggravated assault) declined 32 percent from 1994-98 for youth ages 15-17 and 27 percent for children 14 and under.

Youth remains a period of heightened offending. Both arrest data and self-report surveys show that age 18 is the peak year in life for offending, and that adolescents commit crimes at far higher rates than any group except young adults. The combination of projected growth in the number of adolescents over the next decade and the toxic social conditions that exist today for many children place us in danger of a renewed rise in adolescent crime early in the new century. But ***exaggerated fears and overheated rhetoric will only distract policymakers and citizens from the critical challenge of erecting the better delinquency prevention and juvenile justice systems we need.***

- **Instead of new investments in research and development and broad implementation of proven program models and best practice reforms, political action against youth crime was dominated in the 1990s by new laws to transfer whole classes of adolescent offenders to adult courts and adult corrections. This is the wrong answer to juvenile crime – and should be abandoned at all levels of government.**

Far from reducing crime, experience shows that transfer to criminal (i.e., adult) courts actually increases the future criminality of youthful offenders. In study after study, juvenile offenders who are transferred to criminal court recidivate more often, more quickly, and with more serious offenses than those who are retained under juvenile jurisdiction. In Minnesota, 58 percent of transferred youth committed an additional crime within two years versus 42 percent of youth retained in juvenile courts. A Florida study of more than 5,000 offenders found that transferred youth had a higher re-arrest rate (30 vs. 19 percent) and shorter time period to re-arrest (135 days vs. 227 days) than youth retained in the juvenile justice system. Studies in Pennsylvania and New York report similar findings, and other research proves that the threat of being tried as an adult does not deter youth from crime.

Meanwhile, transfer can expose youth to grave risks. Compared with youth confined in the juvenile justice system, juvenile offenders housed in adult jails and prisons are eight times more likely to commit suicide, five times more likely to be sexually assaulted, twice as likely to be beaten by staff, and 50 percent more likely to be attacked with a weapon. Prisons are, however, a great place for youth to learn the tools of the crime trade from grizzled veterans. Moreover, transfers to criminal court severely damage the life chances of youth by staining them for life with a criminal record. Transfers are especially damaging for minority youth – who make up 77 percent of all youth confined in adult prisons. "Adult time for adult crime" is a catchy phrase, but irresponsible public policy.

- **Our nation's juvenile justice institutions themselves present significant barriers to implementing effective practices that prevent and reverse delinquent behavior. Though a separate, rehabilitation-oriented system of justice remains the only sensible approach for addressing adolescent crime, the operation of juvenile justice is highly problematic in most states and cities.**

Despite stirrings of positive change in some states and localities, most juvenile justice systems continue to devote the great bulk of their resources to confinement of youthful offenders – including many who pose no danger to the community. A 1993 study of 28 states found that only 14 percent of offenders confined in juvenile correctional institutions were committed for serious violent crimes. More than half of the youth in state institutions were committed for property or drug crimes and were serving their first terms in a state institution. Moreover, despite a cost of $100 to $150 per youth per day, delinquents sentenced to youth correctional facilities typically suffer recidivism rates of 50 to 70 percent. A follow-up study on youth released from Minnesota's two correctional "training schools" in 1991 found that 91 percent had been arrested within five years of release. In Maryland, a study of 947 youths released from correctional facilities in 1994 found that 82 percent were referred to juvenile or criminal courts within two and one-half years after release.

Meanwhile, most jurisdictions spend little for home-based, family-oriented, and multi-dimensional rehabilitation strategies that have proven more successful than incarceration in reducing delinquent behavior. Most jurisdictions provide few meaningful responses to the early delinquency of young adolescents, even those at high risk to become chronic offenders. Many pay little attention to results and instead continue to fund many ineffective or counterproductive approaches, rather than replicating methodologies that have been scientifically proven to reduce offending. Meanwhile, unequal treatment of minority youth is pervasive in juvenile justice nationwide, and other violations of adolescents' civil and human rights occur in a disturbing number of states and localities.

- **A new and improved juvenile justice system is necessary but not sufficient to win the battle against juvenile crime. Rather, juvenile justice must be combined with complementary efforts to prevent delinquency before it starts.**

Prevention experts have developed an impressive array of strategies in recent years to preclude the onset of delinquent behaviors and to correct the behavior of pre-adolescent children who display serious conduct problems. Many of the most successful strategies engage parents and improve the home environment of high-risk children. For instance, such early childhood programs as home visits from nurses and enriched pre-school programs for high-rise toddlers have lowered subsequent delinquency by up to 80 percent. Likewise, research-based programs for young children with conduct disorders – providing parenting training for the parents and/or social competency for the children themselves – substantially reduce behavior problems in 70 to 90 percent of cases. Several school-based and community-based prevention strategies have also demonstrated power to reduce delinquent behavior.

Unfortunately, many efforts to prevent delinquency suffer from the same weak focus on results that plagues juvenile justice. For instance, a 1997 study of school-based prevention programming in 19 school districts found that "Districts rarely implemented approaches that, according to current research, have the greatest potential for making a difference for students." Failure to implement proven strategies leads communities to squander many opportunities to avert delinquent careers through targeted early childhood programs, research-driven school-based prevention efforts, community-based youth development, and effective mental health treatment for disturbed children at heightened risk for delinquency.

RECOMMENDATIONS: Meeting the Youth Crime Challenge

Thanks to the unprecedented spree of youth violence in the late 1980s and early '90s, overheated rhetoric about juvenile "superpredators" since the mid-1990s, and horrific school shooting tragedies in Columbine and other communities since 1997, adolescent crime and violence have risen to the top of our nation's policy agenda.

Thanks to our growing understanding about the roots of criminality and our increasing arsenal of effective strategies, America has an opportunity to further reduce juvenile crime and hold it down in the years to come. We know how to improve the success of juvenile justice systems in lowering recidivism among delinquent youth, and we know how to avert the onset of delinquent careers through targeted prevention. Many effective solutions cost far less to implement than current policies and programs.

To capture the opportunities for reform, however, states and communities will have to overcome deep-rooted obstacles. Many state and local policymakers lack information about effective practices. Many agencies have limited capacity to plan and develop new programs effectively, and many lack start-up funding to support the spread of promising practices. Meanwhile, the political environment surrounding youth crime issues remains highly charged – exacerbating the tendency of public leaders to avoid risks and shun the kind of wrenching operational changes that would be required of professionals and agencies to implement many reforms. For understandable reasons, then, the deck is now stacked against reforms urgently needed to hold down youth crime rates in the years to come.

What will it take to overcome these obstacles and begin building positive momentum for progress against adolescent crime? ***While the process will be long and complex, the first step is straightforward: We must elevate the debate over youth crime by rejecting the simplistic formulation of "adult***

Critical Action Steps to Reduce Juvenile Crime

- Provide research-proven treatment and services for young children with behavioral problems and their families.
- Use objective screening criteria to identify youthful offenders at highest risk to re-offend, and work intensively with them.
- Deliver community-based, family-focused treatment for delinquent youth who pose no risk to the community.
- Reduce reliance on correctional training schools and other out-of-home placements for delinquent youth who do not endanger public safety.
- Offer alternatives-to-detention for non-dangerous juvenile offenders awaiting trial.
- Implement "graduated sanctions," including treatment and youth development services, to ensure appropriate, predictable, and proportionate responses whenever delinquent youth commit additional crimes or violate probation.
- Correct justice system biases that perpetuate unequal access to treatment and services as well as disproportionate confinement of minority youth.
- Coordinate services among agencies – juvenile justice, education, mental health and child welfare – that share responsibility for troubled youth.
- Recruit local volunteers and engage community-based organizations to work directly with high-risk and delinquent youth.
- Develop alternative programs like drug courts, teen courts, family-group conferencing, and victim-offender mediation to hold young offenders accountable while connecting them to positive resources in their communities.
- Make quality aftercare a core component of juvenile corrections programs to help youthful offenders make a successful transition back into the community following their confinement.
- Support intensive early childhood intervention programs to promote the healthy development of infants and toddlers in high-risk families.
- Implement effective school-based prevention models.
- Mobilize the entire community to plan and implement comprehensive youth crime prevention strategies that involve families, schools, and neighborhoods.

time for adult crime" and dismissing proposals to disband juvenile courts or further erode their jurisdiction. Overwhelming evidence proves that transferring youth to adult courts exacerbates the criminality of those transferred and fails to deter crime among other youth. Powerful analysis demonstrates that measured punishments, high-quality treatment services, community-based youth development programming, and freedom from a criminal record are far more effective at turning delinquent youth away from crime than criminal prosecution or incarceration with adult convicts.

Hundreds of years after the introduction of Common Law, the United States led the world in 1899 by creating the first court system in history specifically for young people. Today, separate juvenile justice systems operate in virtually every civilized nation on earth. With public concern over youth crime now atop the list of public concerns, ***America should not abandon this home-grown solution. Rather, we must re-embrace the juvenile justice ideal and dedicate ourselves to retooling and reforming our juvenile justice and delinquency prevention systems to meet the demands of a new century.***

Herein lies the more difficult challenge: strengthening and reshaping juvenile justice and delinquency prevention efforts nationwide to capitalize on our rapidly increasing knowledge of what works. Specifically, five areas of strategic action offer the greatest promise:

1. End Over-Reliance on Corrections and Other Out-of-Home Placements for Delinquent Youth. In most states, local juvenile courts face a strong financial incentive to commit troubled youth to state correctional institutions rather than treat them locally – even for youth who pose no threat to public safety. Likewise, most of the costs for placing troubled youth into group homes and residential treatment centers are reimbursed typically with federal, state, or private insurance funds. By contrast, the costs to retain youth at home and provide community-based supervision and treatment are paid entirely by the locality in most states. To reverse this counterproductive dynamic, ***states should revise their funding formulas to reward localities for serving youth in their homes and communities whenever possible and also require localities to pay a share of the costs when they commit non-dangerous youth to state correctional facilities. Likewise, states should reduce unnecessary placements of delinquents and otherwise-troubled youth to group homes and residential treatment centers*** by developing "systems of care" reforms that reward child welfare agencies and other service providers for minimizing over-reliance on out-of-home placements.

2. Invest in Research-Based Interventions for Juvenile Offenders, as well as Research-Based Prevention. The advances produced by delinquency scholars and researchers over the past two decades can revolutionize America's approach to juvenile crime. In fact, the new evidence demands drastic change, because it demonstrates clearly that today's common practices are often ineffective, even counterproductive. Based on these findings, ***the federal government and foundations should invest heavily in the replication and further refinement of effective strategies and in continuing research efforts to develop even better strategies for quelling delinquent conduct among troubled youth.*** Juvenile justice agencies at all levels should invest in the widespread implementation of promising and proven strategies, and they should eliminate or modify strategies that don't work.

3. Measure Results, Fund What Works, and Cut Funds to What Doesn't Work. Substantive information about programs, services, budgets and especially outcomes is hard to come by in most juvenile justice agencies. This scarcity of hard facts presents both a critical problem today and an opportunity to spur meaningful reforms in the future. As noted above, the available evidence shows that many current juvenile justice and delinquency prevention efforts are not effective. Thus, measuring results is critical. ***The federal government should make concrete, standardized evaluation a requirement for all states and localities receiving federal juvenile justice and delinquency prevention funds.*** Given the federal government's central role in research and development, and given its small percentage of the nation's overall juvenile justice and delinquency prevention budgets, developing new knowledge must be a core goal for all federal spending. ***State and local leadership is also critical for data collection and program evaluation. Juvenile justice agencies nationwide should create outcome databases to measure the effectiveness of all juvenile justice programs.*** These data will allow policymakers and the public to clearly identify what is working and what isn't. This information is critical to build momentum for substantive reform of youth crime reduction efforts.

4. Engage Community Partners. Two of the characteristic traits of youth who fall into delinquent lifestyles are lack of attachment to caring adults and lack of involvement in school and other positive, pro-social activities in their communities – an after-school program, a job, church, community service. "Disconnected" youth comprise the lion's share of the delinquency population. In many localities, juvenile courts and juvenile justice agencies also suffer from a "disconnection" problem. While they routinely refer youth to service providers in their communities, many juvenile courts have not formed strong working partnerships with partner agencies, community organizations, or local citizens to help fill in the missing pieces in delinquent youths' lives. ***States should encourage or even require juvenile courts and probation agencies to strengthen partnerships with residents, community-based organizations, and partner agencies. At the local level, juvenile justice leaders must re-connect youth to caring adults and positive activities in their communities through innovative "restorative justice" initiatives such as family-group conferences, community accountability boards, teen courts, drug courts, and Youth Aid Panels; and they should establish multi-agency teams to jointly assess and oversee treatment of high-risk youth involved in the child welfare, education, juvenile justice, and mental health systems.***

5. Mobilize Whole Communities to Study, Plan and Implement Comprehensive Strategies for Combatting Youth Crime. Since 1994, the Office of Juvenile Justice and Delinquency Prevention has provided funds for more than 600 communities to undertake comprehensive planning for new and improved efforts to prevent delinquency and related problem behaviors (such as substance abuse, teen pregnancy, and school failure), and to strengthen local responses when youth do commit crimes. Despite positive results, some proposals are now pending in Congress to eliminate this federal funding stream. ***Congress should reject these proposals and instead continue and expand funding for comprehensive community analysis, planning, and mobilization. With or without federal support, states should emulate the example of states like Kansas, North Carolina, Pennsylvania, and Texas by requiring local jurisdictions to create local policy boards and develop comprehensive community plans. Likewise, localities on their own should mobilize public officials, community leaders and residents to undertake intensive analysis, planning, and program development.***

Americans are right to view youth crime as a major concern for our society. If we are willing to roll up our sleeves and get to work, effective solutions are now available. The time has come for communities and political leaders to rise to this challenge.

Part One: BREAKTHROUGHS

Little noticed in the public and political uproar over juvenile crime in the 1980s and '90s, researchers and practitioners in juvenile justice, delinquency prevention, criminology and behavioral science have made dramatic progress in uncovering the reasons why some youth embrace crime and in devising effective strategies to prevent and curb adolescent criminality.

This work is far from complete. A tremendous amount of research remains to be done. Yet valuable new knowledge is emerging at a rapid rate. Already, we know enough to substantially improve the success of our efforts to reduce delinquency and violence among young people. The following pages review this research, illustrating beyond doubt that our nation has the powerful tools we need to substantially reduce adolescent crime.

Chapter One
WHAT IF?
(A Journey to the State-of-the-Art in Delinquency Prevention and Treatment)

What if we could take a chronic juvenile delinquent, a kid who has been arrested five, six, ten times, and instead of sending him away for a year to juvenile prison for $40,000 or $50,000 (only to come home with a 50 to 70 percent chance of re-offending)... what if instead of that we could keep him at home, spend less than $5,000 working with him and his family over four or five months, and cut the likelihood that he'll re-offend in half?

What if, for a chronic delinquent who is just too unruly to stay with her parents, instead of sending her to a group home or youth prison we could spend just a little more to place her into a specialized foster home for six to nine months, work with the child and coach her parents, and reduce the amount of time she can expect to be incarcerated by 75 days over the next two years?

What if, for chronically disobedient elementary school children, we could spend just $1,500 for a two-pronged program – video-based parenting skills training and classroom-based social competence training for the child – and reduce problem behaviors dramatically (by 30 percent or better) in 95 percent of all cases, significantly reducing the number who will be arrested later as juveniles?

Well, you can stop asking "what if." We can. We can. And we can.

Almost always, however, we don't, we don't, and we don't.

Over the past two decades, scholars and juvenile justice policy innovators have developed the tools our society needs to significantly reduce delinquency. Yet somehow, word of these advances has not reached policymakers or program practitioners – or if it did reach them, they haven't yet taken notice.

What are these dramatic new advances?

First, we have significantly broadened our knowledge about the underlying causes of crime in the lives of individual offenders, as well as the developmental pathways leading to delinquency and crime. Second, we have developed, field-tested, and validated several strategies that markedly improve success in reducing delinquent behavior – both lowering recidivism rates of adolescent offenders and preventing youth from lapsing into delinquency to begin with. Third, through innovation and research by scholars and practitioners, we have identified a set of empirically proven best practices to guide delinquency prevention and juvenile justice systems.

These insights provide our nation the opportunity to dramatically strengthen our campaign against juvenile crime. Consider the three program models below, each of which sharply reduces recidivism among chronic youthful offenders. Two are intensive home-based interventions that work not just with the youth but with his or her whole family to identify and reverse the negative dynamics that propel the young person toward delinquency – be they poor parenting skills, substance abuse, a learning disability, or a tense

Multisystemic Therapy Versus Usual Juvenile Justice Treatment for Serious Adolescent Offenders:*

Results of a Randomized Trial in Simpsonville, SC
59 Weeks After Treatment

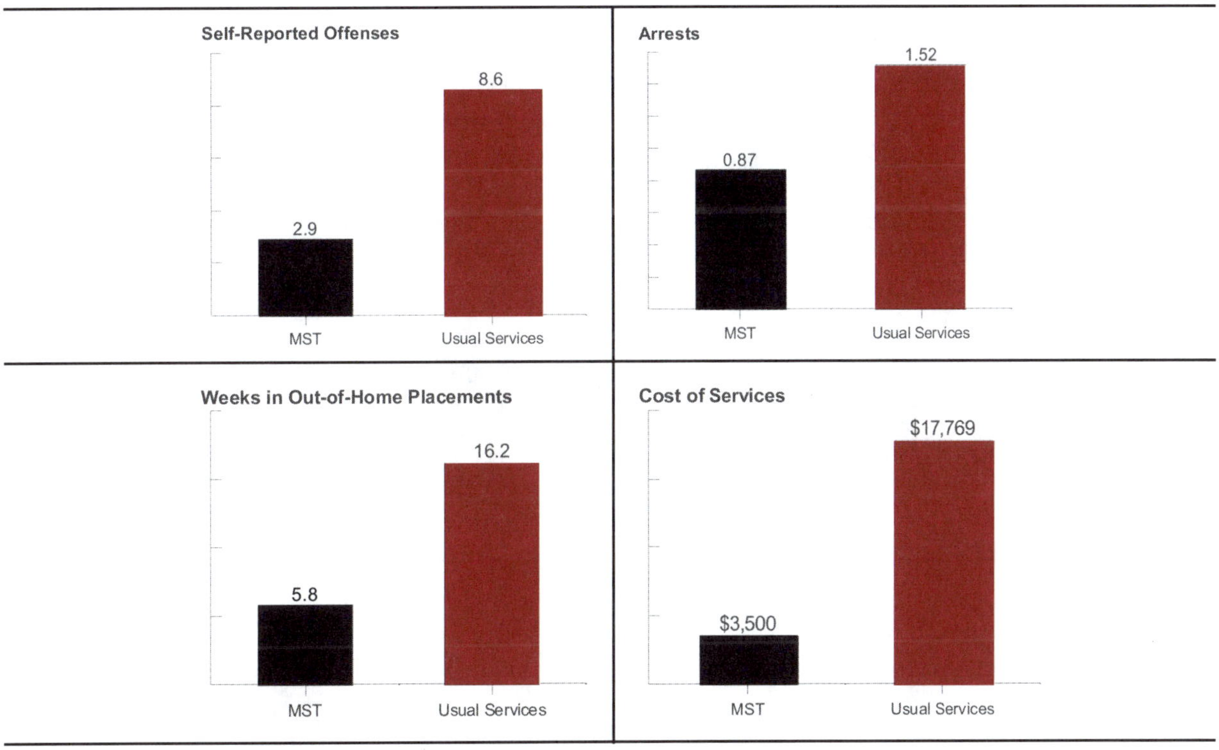

*Profile of Juvenile Offenders Served:
- -- 100% had at least one prior felony arrest
- -- 54% had at least one arrest for a violent crime
- -- Average number of arrests was 3.5 per participant
- -- Participants averaged 9.5 weeks of incarceration
- -- 44% of participants were Caucasian; 56% were African American

Source: Henggeler, S.W., *Treating Serious Anti-Social Behavior in Youth: the MST Approach (Washington, DC: Office of Juvenile Justice and Delinquency Prevention, May 1997).*

step-parent relationship. The therapist engages the family in strategies to overcome these root problems, while at the same time coaching parents in behavior management strategies to begin re-establishing order and respect in the home. The third model places young offenders temporarily into specialized foster homes, works with the youth and simultaneously coaches the parents, and then returns the youth to the home after a six to eight-month treatment period. The results speak for themselves:

- **Multisystemic Therapy**, in which trained therapists work with delinquent youth and their families following an exacting set of principles and procedures, has been examined in eight scientific studies. In each, youth receiving this treatment proved far more successful than youth receiving conventional services. In rural South Carolina, violent and chronic offenders treated with MST had 43 percent fewer arrests, committed 66 percent fewer self-reported offenses, and spent 64 percent fewer weeks in youth prisons or treatment centers than youth randomly assigned to usual court sanctions and treatments (such as court-ordered curfews and school attendance, referral to other community agencies).[1] In Columbia, Missouri, youth who completed MST showed a five-year re-arrest rate of 22.1 percent – less than one-third that of youth who completed individual therapy (71.4 percent). In two other clinical studies, MST reduced days spent in out-of-home placements by 47 percent and 50 percent compared with youth treated in traditional programs.[2] Multisystemic Therapy costs

Functional Family Therapy Versus Alternative Treatments: Recidivism Results of Four Evaluation Studies

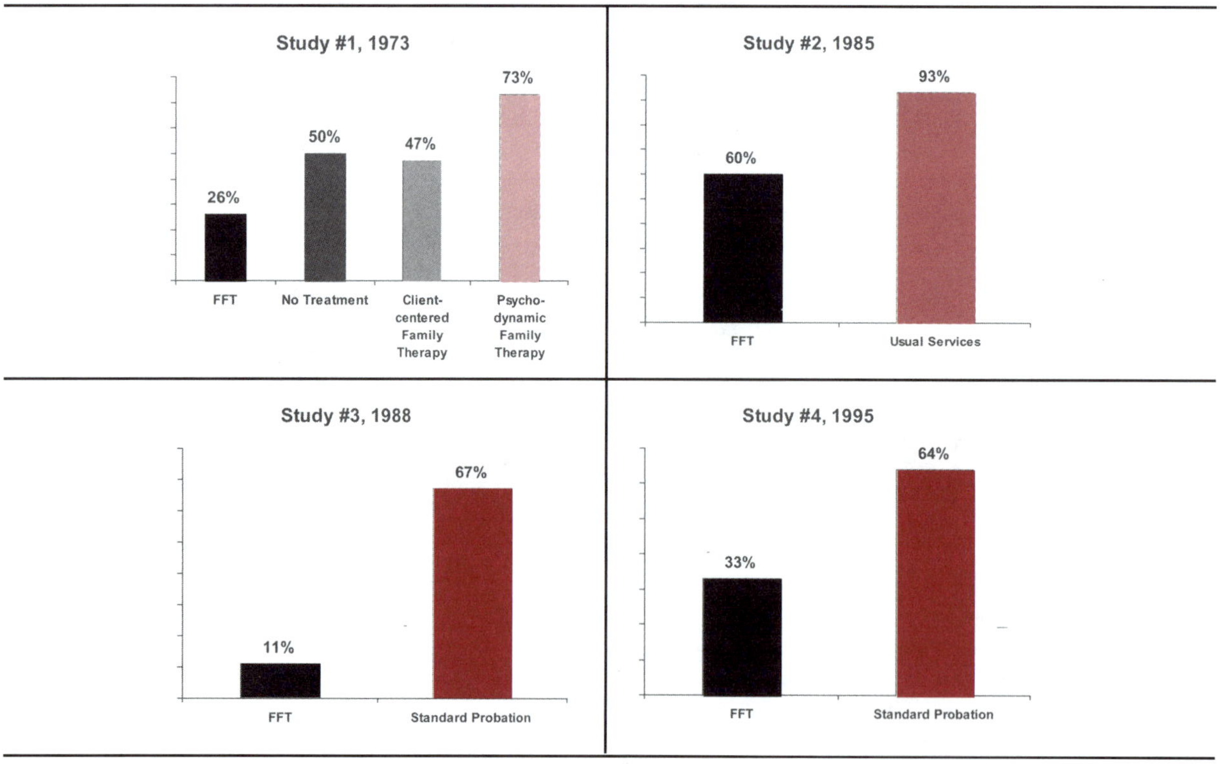

Source: All Studies cited in Alexander, James F., *Blueprint for Violence Prevention Book Three: Functional Family Therapy* (Boulder, CO: Center for the Study and Prevention of Violence, 1998).

only $4,500 per youth, far less than incarceration or placement into a group home.

- Like Multisystemic Therapy, **Functional Family Therapy** works with youth in their homes and targets both the family and the individual behavior of the youth – employing intensive and research-driven tactics to identify and reverse the negative dynamics that produce problem behaviors. Functional Family Therapy first demonstrated its impact way back in 1973, when a randomized trial found that only 26 percent of delinquent youth assigned to FFT were arrested within 18 months of treatment, compared with 50 percent recidivism for youth in a no-treatment control group, and 47 percent and 73 percent recidivism for youth assigned to two other modes of therapy.[3] In another trial with serious and chronic youthful offenders, participants in FFT were almost six times as likely to avoid arrest (40 percent vs. 7 percent) than a control group.[4] Overall, between 1973 and 1997, FFT was involved in nine scientific studies, and in every test FFT produced improvement of at least 25 percent (and up to 80 percent) in recidivism, out-of-home placement, or future offending by siblings of treated youth.[5] Functional Family Therapy costs even less than MST – just $2,000 per youth.

Multidimensional Treatment Foster Care versus Placement into Group Homes: Results of a Randomized Trial for Chronic Juvenile Offenders

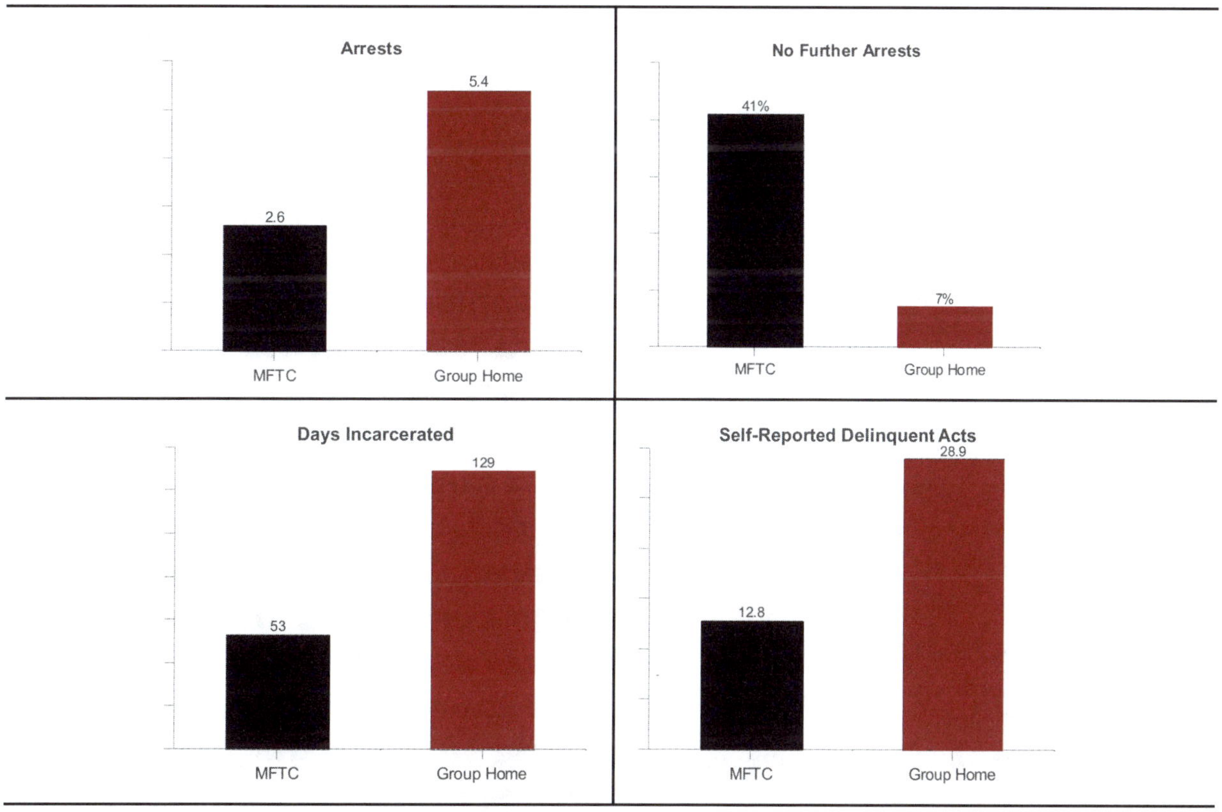

Population: 79 delinquent boys ages 12-17 with an average of 13 prior arrests and 4.6 felony arrests.

Source: Chamberlain, Patricia. *Blueprints for Violence Prevention, Book Eight: Multidimensional Treatment Foster Care* (Boulder, CO: Center for the Study and Prevention of Violence, 1998).

- Developed by the Oregon Social Learning Center, **Multidimensional Treatment Foster Care** provides an alternative to placement into corrections or a "group home" – to which many troubled youth are sent as a last chance before commitment to corrections. In one clinical trial with serious and chronic youthful offenders, those placed in treatment foster care proved twice as likely to complete the program (and not run away), and spent an average of 75 fewer days incarcerated over the subsequent two-year period.[6] In a second trial, those in multidimensional treatment foster care were arrested less than half as often as youth sent to group homes (2.6 vs. 5.4 arrests). They also spent less than half as many days incarcerated and were seven times as likely to remain arrest free in the year after treatment (41 percent to seven percent).[7]

When a team of researchers at the Washington State Institute for Public Policy analyzed the cost-effectiveness of successful crime prevention program models in 1998, they found that ***Functional Family Therapy saved taxpayers $6.85 for every dollar spent in justice system costs alone. Multisystemic Therapy saved taxpayers $8.38 for every dollar spent, and Multidimensional Treatment Foster Care saved $14.07 for each dollar spent.***[8] In fact, these justice systems costs are just the beginning of the savings when programs prevent a youth from sliding into a delinquent lifestyle. When Vanderbilt University Economist Mark Cohen calculated the total cost to society when a single young person drops out of high school and gets involved with drugs and crime, he found that the bill came to $2 million. (See Appendix II.)

New Knowledge On Youth Crime and Its Causes.

The success of these program models – and the many other successful programs and strategies detailed later in this chapter – rests upon a growing foundation of knowledge about the causes and correlates of crime, as well as the developmental pathways leading toward criminality. This research provides the basis for promising strategies to spread success in juvenile crime reduction. Several critical lessons emerge:

- *Only a small percentage of youth become chronic juvenile offenders.*

In 1972, Marvin Wolfgang and his colleagues at the University of Pennsylvania published a seminal study entitled *Delinquency in a Birth Cohort*, which tracked the delinquency and criminal behavior among ten thousand young people born in Philadelphia in 1945 throughout childhood, adolescence and young adulthood.[9] Wolfgang repeated the analysis with more than 25,000 youth born in 1958, and in recent years several more cohort studies have been conducted by other criminologists.[10] This research provides a window into the onset and course of delinquent and criminal careers, replacing centuries of speculation with hard data about who commits crime, when, and under what conditions. Perhaps the most important finding of these studies is that a small group of boys – just six to eight percent – commit the majority of all serious and violent

[New] research provides a window into the onset and course of delinquent and criminal careers, replacing centuries of speculation with hard data about who commits crime, when, and under what conditions. Perhaps the most important finding of these studies is that a small group of boys – just six to eight percent – commit the majority of all serious and violent juvenile crimes.

juvenile crimes. For instance, Wolfgang's second analysis found that seven percent of Philadelphia youth committed 61 percent of all offenses, 65 percent of all aggravated assaults, 60 percent of homicides, 75 percent of rapes, and 73 percent of robberies.[11] Girls' offending rates have increased rapidly in recent years, presenting the juvenile justice system with a critical challenge. However, girls remain far less likely than boys to engage in violence or become chronic offenders. ***To be effective in reducing youth crime, prevention and intervention efforts must target those young people at highest risk to become chronic offenders.***

- *Criminal careers almost always begin in childhood.*

According to Delbert Elliott, whose National Youth Survey tracked the delinquent and criminal careers of 1,725 youth through age 27, "Serious violent offending begins essentially between the ages of 12 and 20. The risk of initiation is close to 0 after age 20."[12] Likewise, the onset of chronic and violent offending during youth is almost always preceded by defiant, disruptive, aggressive and other problem behavior during childhood. ***Youth-oriented crime prevention efforts that identify and intervene effectively with high-risk children offer a potentially invaluable avenue for reducing crime.***

- *Those who become serious, chronic, or violent criminals typically follow predictable developmental pathways.*

Rolf Loeber at the University of Pittsburgh has identified three distinct pathways children follow on their way to becoming chronic delinquents and then adult criminals: an *overt pathway* (leading from bullying and other aggression during childhood, to physical fighting in early adolescence, to serious violence); a *covert pathway* (leading from shoplifting and frequent lying, to vandalism and/or fire-setting, to serious property crimes); and an *authority conflict pathway* (leading from stubbornness to defiance to truancy and other rule-breaking, to serious delinquency in the form of violent and/or property offending). Between 80 and 90 percent of youths who become chronic delinquents follow one or more of these pathways.[13] ***Understanding these pathways provides an opportunity to identify high-risk children and youth and to intervene early to deter the potential onset of criminality.***

- *Increasingly, scholars tie the onset or prevention of delinquency to common "risk factors" that heighten youths' propensity toward conduct problems, and to common "protective factors" that can insulate youth against these risks.*

During the 1980s and '90s, a unifying theory emerged to explain why young people turn to delinquency, and why they desist or persist in delinquency over time. This "Social Development Model" rests upon two pillars: ***risk*** and ***protection***. Bridging the age-old divide in criminology pitting "root causes" theorists (who tend to explain criminality as an inevitable consequence of injustice and inequality in society) and "individual responsibility" adherents (who place all blame for crime at the hands of offenders), "Social Development" focuses on both individual and environmental variables with proven connections to offending.

. . . exposure to violence, drugs, guns, street gangs, and concentrated poverty substantially increase the likelihood that a young person will become delinquent . . .

- **In the community,** exposure to violence, drugs, guns, street gangs, and concentrated poverty substantially increase the likelihood that a young person will become delinquent, while participation in positive community activities and connection to caring adults can reduce the risk of delinquency even for youth in the most troubled neighborhoods.

- **At school,** risks include early academic failure, weak attachment to school, and a poor school environment, while protective factors include academic success, motivation to learn, and a positive school climate;
- **With peers,** the risk factors include connection to gangs or other deviant or anti-social peer groups, while protective factors include connection to positive and pro-social peers;
- **In the family,** risk factors include parental abuse or neglect, family history of substance abuse or criminality, frequent family conflict, and neglectful or overly harsh parenting while protective factors include consistent and supportive parental supervision and strong attachment to one or both parents; and
- **Within the individual,** the risk factors include early conduct problems, abuse of drugs or alcohol, mental health problems, rebelliousness, impulsiveness, and poor social problem-solving skills, while protective factors include a resilient temperament, positive outlook, and an orientation to the future.

Serious delinquency and other negative youth behaviors do not derive from any single cause. Rather, bad outcomes arise when multiple risk factors in the school, family, and community combine with an individual child's propensity toward delinquency. In this light, preventing delinquency becomes an effort to minimize children's exposure to dangerous risk factors and to maximize the protective factors in their lives. ***Delinquency prevention succeeds when intervention efforts correctly identify the risk factors that propel individual young people toward crime, and when they target those risks or counteract them with positive influences.***

- *More and more, research shows that the family is the most important factor both in triggering the onset of delinquent behaviors and in bringing delinquent behavior under control.*

"There is no single cause of youth violence, but when there is a common factor that cuts across different cases, it is usually some kind of family dysfunction," Temple University psychologist Lawrence Steinberg told a working group on youth violence in the U.S. House of Representatives in September 1999.[14] Steinberg identified six avenues through which family problems can lead to delinquency and violence: ***exposure to violence in the home***, which makes violence more acceptable in the eyes of youth as a means to solve problems; ***biological changes in the brain***, which have been detected in children exposed to violence and trauma during early childhood; ***mental health problems***, which are prevalent in children whose parents are hostile, punitive, or neglectful; ***personality problems***, which often develop in children raised by negative or erratic parents; ***academic problems***, which arise often among children whose parents do not take an active and constructive interest in their education; and ***susceptibility to negative peer pressure***, as parents fail to supervise their children's behavior, and the peer group (or gang) becomes a powerful and anti-social influence. Reporting on his research with a sample of 20,000 teenagers, Steinberg told the House working group that "By far the adolescents who had the greatest number of problems – not just with antisocial behavior, but also in school, in personality development, and in general mental health, came from families in which parents were hostile aloof, or uninvolved."[15] ***Delinquency prevention and intervention efforts that ignore the family context, or address family issues only***

"By far the adolescents who had the greatest number of problems – not just with antisocial behavior, but also in school, in personality development, and in general mental health, came from families in which parents were hostile aloof, or uninvolved."

marginally, are unlikely to produce lasting change in the behavior of delinquent and at-risk youth.

- *As young people enter adolescence, connections to delinquent peers can escalate the risks for offending markedly.*

When adults commit theft, rape, robbery, homicide, burglary, or assault, they usually act alone. When adolescents commit any of these crimes, they usually do so in the company of other youth. "No fact of adolescent criminality is more important than what sociologists call 'group context,'" writes University of California at Berkeley criminologist Franklin Zimring.[16] While the influence of peer pressure on adolescents is not a new finding, the full importance of peer factors in delinquency prevention is only now coming to light. In September 1999, the journal *American Psychologist* published an article examining two intervention programs for delinquent youth that worked with some youth in groups and others individually. In both cases, youth who participated heavily in the group activities not only had higher recidivism than those who took part in more individualized and family treatments, but they also had higher recidivism than control group youth receiving no intervention.[17] ***More than one-fourth of delinquency prevention and treatment programs evaluated in recent years have shown counterproductive results. Many of the unsuccessful programs – as well as virtually all programs operating today in correctional settings, residential treatment centers and group homes – utilize group approaches that bring delinquent youth together with their troubled peers. The evidence suggests that many or most of these youth would be better served in programs that minimize rather than mandate interaction among delinquent peers.***

- *Most young people who commit crimes during adolescence terminate their delinquency by the time they reach adulthood.*

More than 30 percent of boys examined in the National Youth Survey committed one or more acts of serious violence by age 18. Few of these youth were ever arrested for violent offenses, but more than three-fourths nonetheless terminated their violence by age 21. Other research has found that the criminal careers of most violent juvenile offenders span only a single year. ***Understanding this self-correcting dynamic is crucial in any attempt to combat juvenile crime. Most juvenile offenders – even those who commit serious acts of violence – are not destined for lives of crime.*** Instead, they

Advances in theory and practice in juvenile crime prevention offer America the opportunity to take a giant step forward in our fight to control adolescent crime. Unfortunately, most citizens in our nation – and most policymakers as well – remain unaware of the potential for progress. Funding for replication of model programs and for policy reforms based on research-proven principles are moving at a snail's pace.

Some youth are too dangerous to remain out on the streets. Some have no safe and healthy place to go home to. Some have committed crimes so heinous or offended so chronically that society's moral standards demand serious punishment. These youth require out-of-home placement. Yet for the majority of youthful offenders, including many who are currently locked inside correctional youth facilities, success would be far more likely through supervision, treatment services, and youth development opportunities in their own homes and communities.

are teenagers exercising bad judgement – sometimes catastrophic judgement – succumbing to peer pressure and temporarily losing control. These youth should be punished for their crimes, but punished in ways that do not seriously damage their future life chances.

- *America is actually suffering two adolescent crime problems, adolescence-limited offending by otherwise "normal" youth who slip into bad behaviors for a brief period of their youth, and crime committed by those who will go on to become life-long offenders.*

Terrie Moffitt at the University of Wisconsin has found that a similar percentage of the male population (roughly 3-6 percent) demonstrates acute behavioral problems at many stages of life – difficult temperaments in early childhood, conduct disorders in elementary school, early arrest in pre-adolescence, violent crime arrest by age 20, and adult diagnosis of antisocial personality disorder. By contrast, Moffitt reported, 20 to 25 percent of teenage males are arrested between the ages of 15 and 18.[18] As noted above, more than three-fourths of youth who commit violent offenses during adolescence "age out" of these behaviors by age 21. The key difference between those who desist from crime and those who continue is that desisters succeed in forming positive connections with the mainstream society – finding steady above-board work, a life partner, or both. That is why our ***youth crime policies must optimize rather than damage youths' chances to make positive connections during young adulthood. In our zeal to punish, we will only exacerbate the crime problem if we further alienate youthful offenders from society, damage their opportunities to "make it" in the mainstream, and fail to help them develop the arsenal of practical and social skills necessary to make it.***

Advances in Community-Based Treatment of Juvenile Offenders.

If there is one clear finding to be gleaned from the research on juvenile justice programming in recent decades, it is that removing youthful offenders from their homes is often not a winning strategy for reducing long-term delinquency. Most juvenile corrections facilities, residential treatment centers, and therapeutic group homes suffer very high recidivism rates. Intensive community-based supervision programs typically produce recidivism rates as low or lower than out-of-home placement (at a fraction of the cost), while intensive family-focused or multi-dimensional intervention programs have produced the lowest recidivism rates of all.

Some youth are too dangerous to remain out on the streets. Some have no safe and healthy place to go home to. Some have committed crimes so heinous or offended so chronically that society's moral standards demand serious punishment. These youth require out-of-home placement. Yet for the majority of youthful offenders, including many who are currently locked inside correctional youth facilities, success would be far more likely through supervision, treatment services, and youth development opportunities in their own homes and communities.

This fact flies in the face of current juvenile justice practices throughout most of our nation. It also presents a tremendous opportunity for juvenile justice policy reform. ***Roughly two-thirds of all dollars now spent on juvenile justice go to housing delinquent youth in institutional settings outside their family homes – with costs ranging from $100 to over $200 per youth per day. The majority of the youth removed from their homes are not violent or chronic felony offenders. For far less money, juvenile justice innovators have demonstrated that we can supervise these young offenders in the community, keep most of them crime-free, and reduce the likelihood that they will offend again in the future.***

Developing Non-Residential Sanctions and Services. In addition to Multisystemic Therapy and Functional Family Therapy, two of the powerful models highlighted at the outset of this chapter, several other intensive non-residential treatment and youth development strategies are also proving highly effective. **Structural Family Therapy**, developed by Jose Szapocznik at the University of Miami, has also dramatically reduced problem behaviors among troubled children and adolescents. In the late 1980s, Szapocznik conducted a three-way experiment with 6-11 year-old Hispanic children with acute behavior problems. Szapocznik found that children receiving Structural Family Therapy or conventional individual counseling achieved roughly equivalent success during treatment, and both groups significantly outperformed a no-treatment group (receiving only recreation activities). However, one year after treatment the individual therapy group suffered significantly more problems and experienced a deterioration in family functioning, while family functioning in the structural family therapy group continued to improve. "Treating only the child appears to sufficiently treat the symptom," Szapocznik concluded, "but neglects and increases risk for family functioning."[19] In a 2000 study, Structural Family Therapy proved far more successful than group counseling for 12-18 year-old Hispanic adolescents with behavior problems. Nearly half of the structural family therapy participants with severe conduct disorders made substantial improvements, compared to only five percent of group therapy youth. Likewise, youth receiving structural family therapy were three times as likely to reduce their aggression.[20]

Multidimensional Family Therapy, another model, has also shown strong impact in reversing behavior problems among troubled youth, particularly those with substance abuse problems. In a 1996 study of drug-abusing adolescents, this intervention improved parenting skills in 69 percent of the participating families. In addition, 71 percent of participating youth significantly reduced "acting out" behaviors and 79 percent significantly reduced their substance use.[21] In another study, hard drug use declined from 53 percent of participating youth at the outset of the program, to nine percent at the end of the treatment period, to three percent at one-year follow-up.[22] A third study found that substance abuse declined 55 percent during the treatment period and maintained the low level at 12-month follow-up, whereas group therapy produced only a 37 percent decline and multi-family education yielded only a 25 percent decline.

So-called **"wraparound services"** offer another promising model for community-based treatment of delinquent offenders and other troubled youth. Emerging in the 1980s as a strategy to minimize out-of-home (and especially out-of-state)

Wraparound Milwaukee: Impact on Offending Rates

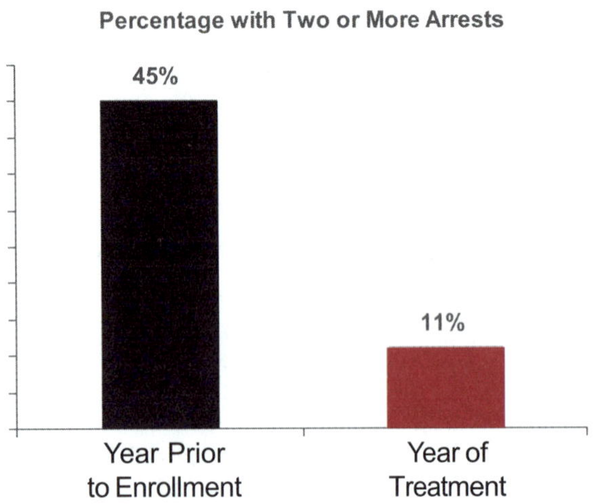

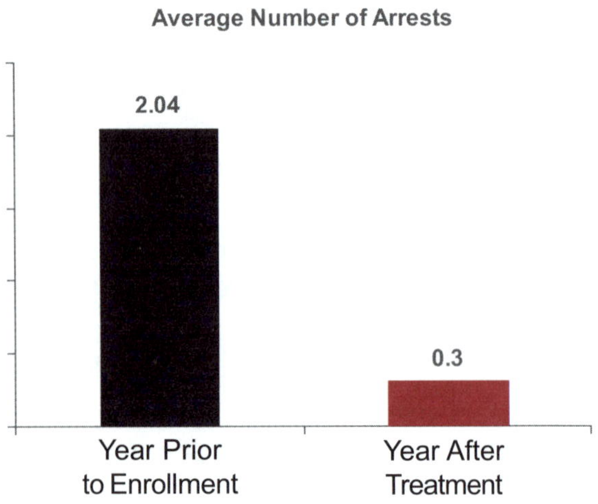

Source: Milwaukee County Health Division

placement of troubled youth into group homes or residential treatment centers, wraparound services are designed to "wrap" individualized services and supports around the individual, rather than forcing the young person to fit into a pre-determined program in an artificial environment. Each young person is assigned a care coordinator who provides mentoring support and leads a process to assess the needs of the young person, work with his or her family, identify and coordinate needed services, and maintain close supervision.

In some communities, wraparound has served as the hub of comprehensive systems reform to coordinate all agencies working with emotionally troubled youth – including child welfare, mental health, special education, and juvenile justice. **Wraparound Milwaukee**, a $27 million project serving 600 young people each year, provides trained care coordinators who arrange needed services through dozens of providers citywide. With funding from Medicaid, mental health, and juvenile justice, Wraparound Milwaukee receives a flat monthly fee for each participant and must pay for all costs of treatment – including residential care or incarceration. Thus the incentive is strong to help as many youth as possible remain in their homes.[23] U.S. Surgeon General David Satcher praised Wraparound Milwaukee in 1999 and endorsed its managed-care "capitated rate" financing approach as a valuable tool "to ensure that the most appropriate services are purchased" for emotionally disturbed youth and that "long-term, complex care can be offered in an efficient way that reduces costs for all of the involved children and youth agencies."[24]

The Milwaukee program is demonstrating powerful results with a difficult population. Sixty-nine percent of court-ordered participants in 1999 were delinquent offenders, and 72 percent were diagnosed with conduct disorder or oppositional defiance disorder. Yet once treatment began, all clinical behavior measures showed improvement and arrest rates plummeted. Whereas 45 percent of participants had committed two or more offenses in the year prior to enrollment, only 11 percent of participants committed two or more offenses during the year of treatment. Among 54 youth for whom one-year follow-up data were available in April 2000, the average number of arrests declined 85 percent – from 2.04 during the year prior to enrollment to .30 arrests during the year after discharge from the program.[25]

While not as successful as the interventions above, other intensive non-residential programs for juvenile offenders have also demonstrated favorable results. In the late 1980s, the Wayne County, Michigan juvenile court randomly assigned repeat juvenile offenders either to incarceration in a juvenile training school or to one of three non-residential intensive probation programs where offenders received treatment services or counseling while remaining in their own homes and communities. Evaluators found that incarcerated youth were slightly less likely to re-offend than youth in intensive probation; however, this difference was explained by their reduced opportunities for offending while incarcerated – not improved behavior following incarceration. After release, crimes committed by previously incarcerated youth were more likely to be serious and/or violent than those committed by youth placed into intensive probation. ***Intensive probation was "as effective as incarceration at less than one-third the cost," the evaluators concluded.[26] Overall, the project saved taxpayers an estimated $8.8 million over three years.***

Intervening Early With Young High-Risk Offenders. One of the most consistent findings of delinquency research is that youth who initiate delinquent behavior patterns and/or get arrested at an early age are at extremely high risk to become chronic offenders. Among young people participating in the National Youth Survey, for instance, those whose delinquency began before age 12 were two to three times as likely to become chronic offenders as youth who initiated delinquency later in adolescence.

In Orange County, California, probation staff are demonstrating the wisdom of identifying potential chronic offenders early. Examining the characteristics of its delinquency population, Orange County determined that just 8 percent of all youth ever arrested become chronic juvenile offenders. Probing further, they identified traits that predicted most of these chronic offenders at their first offense – age at first arrest, plus the presence of multiple risk factors in family discord, school failure, substance abuse, and pre-delinquent behavior. Based on these data, the County initiated an intensive intervention program in 1994 specifically for youth age 15 or younger at first offense who displayed multiple risk factors. Preliminary results show this "8 Percent Solution" program significantly lowers recidivism rates. In the initial pilot, 49 percent of extreme-risk offenders were adjudicated in the 12 months after entering the program, compared with an historic rate of 93 percent for youth with the same profile.[27] More recently, Orange County has randomly assigned extreme-risk youth either to the "8 Percent" program or to usual probation services. After one year, 20 percent of the "8 percent" treatment youth had been arrested two or more times, compared with 43 percent of usual services youth. Moreover, youth enrolled in the "8 Percent" treatment were far less likely to abuse substances.[28] Similar early intervention initiatives are now being tested in seven other California jurisdictions.

Embracing Restorative Justice. For less-than-dangerous youthful offenders, there is now movement in many states and localities to enhance juvenile probation budgets and expand the menu of community-based services – often involving

"8 Percent Solution" Early Intervention Program for Young, High-Risk Juvenile Offenders

Orange County, California

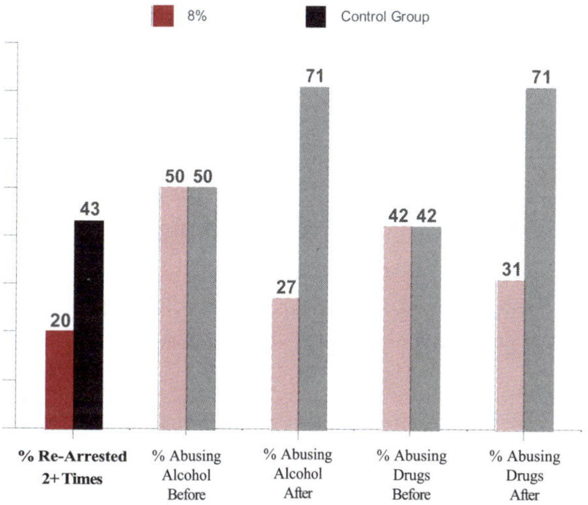

Source: Orange County Probation Department

community volunteers and sometimes requiring youth to meet with victims and take responsibility for the damages they've caused.

- Based on a tradition of the Maori people of New Zealand, **Family Group Conferencing** has been employed to address delinquent behavior in Australia, England, Canada, and several jurisdictions in the United States. In this process, non-violent juvenile offenders meet with their families, victims, and other concerned adults to discuss the cause of the delinquent event and determine a just and fair sanction that will undo the harm caused by the offense. Likewise, **Peacemaking Circles**, a Native American tradition, are also being adopted by many community organizations to address juvenile offending and heal the wounds caused by the offense.

- More and more jurisdictions are creating **"Juvenile Drug Courts"** to work with young offenders troubled by alcohol and drug abuse. These programs, which provide treatment services and extensive individual attention for participating youth, have grown from half a dozen nationwide in 1995 to 90 in 2000 with 72 more in the planning phase.[29]

- "**Teen Courts**," in which young people help determine sentences for other youth, have grown from 50 nationwide in 1991 to 400-500 in 1998.[30] Most teen court cases involve non-violent first offenders who have admitted to committing delinquent acts, and the purpose of the court process is to develop appropriate sentences – typically community service, perhaps combined with victim apology letters, drug/alcohol classes, and/or monetary restitution.

- To reduce gun carrying among adolescents, several jurisdictions nationwide have developed juvenile **"Gun Courts"** or **gun awareness programs** to heighten sensitivity of young first- and second-time weapons offenders to the damage caused by guns and impress on these youth the dangers of carrying a gun.[31]

In Philadelphia, **Youth Aid Panels** comprised of trained community volunteers hear the cases of 800 first-time juvenile offenders every year – 10 percent of all cases referred to juvenile court. Initially established by the Philadelphia District Attorney's Office in 1987, these panels operate in all 24 of Philadelphia's police districts and include ten volunteers each. Panels meet two evenings each month and hear the cases of two juvenile offenders per night – each of whom has admitted to the offense ahead of time. At the hearing, panelists interview the offender, his or her parent(s), and any victims – first reviewing the offense itself and then assessing other positive and negative influences in the offender's life at home, in school, and on the streets.

Unlike the legalistic, rapid-fire, impersonal hearings typical in juvenile court, Youth Aid Panel hearings are deliberate and highly personalized – requiring the young person (and not an attorney) to answer a long series of questions. At the end of the hearing, the panel proposes a three-month "youth aid contract" that might include restitution if the youth has stolen or destroyed property, community service, counseling, Saturday conflict resolution classes, or other requirements. Each offender is also assigned to one of the ten panelists, who then monitors the contract and continues checking in on the young person throughout the three-month period.[32]

Youth Aid Panels and the other models listed above are part of a larger "balanced and restorative justice" movement that strives to enable youth to address the causes of their delinquent behavior and/or to repair the damage done by their offenses. At the same time, youth receive individual attention and become connected to positive influences and activities in their communities. ***More and more, programs are requiring youth to meet with victims and take responsibility for the damages they've caused, and often they provide opportunity for delinquent youth to perform work or provide restitution that enables offenders to earn forgiveness, develop skills, and earn the too-rare satisfaction of performing a valued function in the community.*** "Like all youths, delinquent adolescents need to gain a sense of belonging or connectedness, a sense of usefulness," write Gordon Bazemore and Clinton Terry, two of the leading proponents of this "Restorative Justice" approach.[33]

Though there is limited evaluation data measuring the long-term impact of most "restorative justice" strategies, the trend is encouraging. In Philadelphia, 80 percent of young people participating in Youth Aid Panels complete their contracts successfully. (Those who fail are referred back to the District Attorney for adjudication in juvenile court.) Despite the fact that Youth Aid Panels hear cases of felons as well as misdemeanor offenders, Assistant District Attorney Mike Cleary reports that the recidivism rate of participating youth is only 22 percent.[34] In Washington, D.C., an evaluation of the juvenile drug court found that participants had a 35 percent lower arrest rate than youth assigned to the existing juvenile court.[35]

"Like all youths, delinquent adolescents need to gain a sense of belonging or connectedness, a sense of usefulness."

Reforming Juvenile Detention. For many juvenile offenders, the first step into the juvenile justice system is a stay at a juvenile detention center, the equivalent of a local jail for young people pending trial. These detention centers hold about 25,000 young people nationwide on any given day, and cost $1 billion per year to operate. A number of demonstration and reform efforts have shown that detention populations can be reduced substantially, saving millions of dollars without increasing risks to citizens in the community.

In 1987, Broward County, Florida's juvenile detention center was overflowing, with an average daily population of 160 young offenders. Youth advocacy organizations filed suit to protest the overcrowded conditions, and the County responded by launching a multi-pronged detention reform initiative. It introduced an objective screening device to determine whether each offender was a danger to himself or others, or a risk to flee, and it only detained those who met one of those two criteria. The County created new procedures to minimize "failures to appear" for court hearings, a major problem in Broward (and many other juvenile courts) and a cause for youth to be rounded up and detained. And Broward launched alternatives-to-detention programs to provide intensive oversight as well as mentoring and case-management services for higher-risk youth released pending trial. Through these efforts, Broward County reduced its average daily headcount by two-thirds over five years – to only 56 young people per day – and the County saved $5.2 million in operating costs, construction, and overtime.[36]

The **Detention Diversion Advocacy Program** in San Francisco targets serious youth offenders who are likely to be held in detention prior to trial. The program works with these youth, their families, teachers and other concerned adults to develop a plan for monitoring the young person and for providing needed services to address underlying problems in the young person's life. If the plan is approved by the juvenile judge, which occurs 80 to 90 percent of the time, the young person is released to the custody of the DDAP program. Then program staff phone or see participants every day, arrange needed services, and serve as case managers to ensure that these services are provided. Eighty percent of DDAP youth remain crime-free and attend their hearings. These successful youth are all sentenced to probation when their cases are heard rather than a correctional training school or other out-of-home placement.[37] A 1997 evaluation of DDAP revealed that participants showed an overall recidivism rate barely half as high (34 percent vs. 60 percent) as a comparison group of non-participating youth with similar offending histories. DDAP youth proved only one-third as likely (9 percent vs. 25 percent) to return to court on a violent crime charge and barely one-fourth as likely (14 percent vs. 50 percent) to have two or more subsequent juvenile court referrals.[38]

Detention Diversion Advocacy Program
San Francisco, California

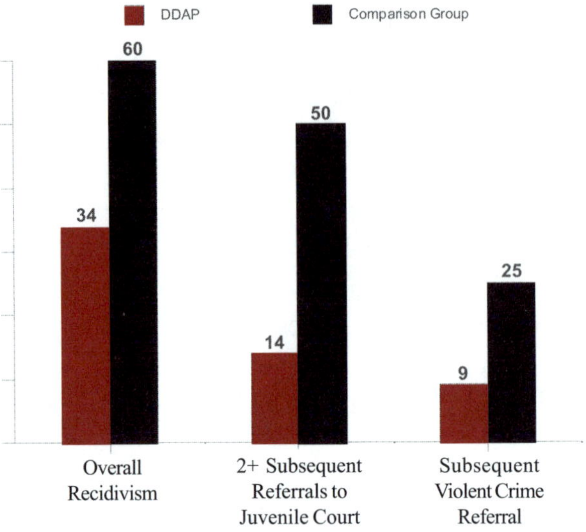

Source: Shelden, Randall, G., *Detention Diversion Advocacy: An Evaluation* (Washington, DC: Office of Juvenile Justice and Delinquency Prevention, September 1999).

Re-Inventing Juvenile Corrections.

Despite high recidivism rates, locked correctional facilities will always have an important place in juvenile justice. Public safety demands it, and experience shows that well-designed, well-operated correctional facilities and programs can reduce future lawbreaking. Studies have repeatedly found that a stay in juvenile corrections tends to slow down the frequency of offending by highly delinquent youth – even if it seldom terminates their offending entirely.[39] Moreover, some correctional facilities enable a far higher percentage of young people to avoid re-arrest after release than traditional training schools.

The Florida Environmental Institute, also known as the "Last Chance Ranch," serves some of Florida's most serious juvenile offenders (average 18 prior offenses and 11.5 felonies) on a remote campus in the Everglades. The program has a low offender-to-staff ratio and uses a three-step rehabilitative process: 1) a work and education phase, in which participants earn points for meeting education and work objectives; 2) an intermediate phase, in which youth participate in paid work projects to help make restitution payments; and 3) an intensive "aftercare" phase during which youth return to their homes and communities but observe a strict curfew and maintain frequent contact with Last Chance Ranch staff. A 1992 study of graduates from the Last Chance Ranch and six other correctional programs found that only 36 percent of graduates returned to juvenile court in the year after release compared with 47 percent to 73 percent for the other six programs.[40] Over the past three years (1997-1999), one-year recidivism by Last Chance Ranch graduates has ranged from 15 to 29 percent – far below that of most correctional programs.[41]

In Texas, the Capital Offender Program works with many of the state's most serious juvenile offenders in a five-month program of intensive group therapy, family counseling (when possible), and post-release monitoring and support. Aimed at pushing youth to take responsibility for their actions while building their empathy and social skills, the program differs markedly from adult prisons. "A kid [who commits a serious crime] could spend 40 years [in adult prison] and never have to talk with a single person about what they did and who they hurt," says Judy Briscoe of the Texas Youth Commission. In the

A 1992 study of graduates from the Last Chance Ranch and six other correctional programs found that only 36 percent of graduates returned to juvenile court in the year after release compared with 47 percent to 73 percent for the other six programs.

Capital Offender Program, "they have to do that from the very first day and again every time they're in a group session. It's a lot more difficult."[42] It is also more effective, data show. Only 5.9 percent of youth participating in the Capital Offender Program were re-arrested on a violent charge within one year – less than half the rate for Texas youth with similar records who did not participate. Likewise, a specialized treatment program for sex offenders has also reduced re-offending.[43]

A critical component in both the Last Chance Ranch and Texas Capital Offender programs is intensive assistance for youth as they re-integrate into the community. Increasingly, experts agree that "aftercare" is a crucial component in effective corrections. However, building strong aftercare programs has proven extremely difficult in most jurisdictions due both to inadequate funding and splintered responsibilities among parole officers, probation staff, judges and community youth agencies. In fact, several experimental aftercare projects have failed to reduce recidivism – in each case because the services envisioned by project designers were never provided. In the late 1980s, for example, the federal Office of Juvenile Justice and Delinquency Prevention funded a Violent Juvenile Offenders project in Memphis, Newark, Boston and Detroit. The model included incarceration in small secure correctional facilities, followed by placement into community-based residential programs (such as group homes), followed by intensive support and supervision after release. In Memphis and Newark, where evaluators found that the model was implemented poorly, recidivism did not improve. However, in Boston and Detroit where it was well-implemented the Violent Juvenile Offender participants had significantly lower recidivism rates, committed less serious crimes, and recidivated less quickly than youth randomly assigned to traditional incarceration.[44]

Winning Strategies to Prevent Delinquency Before it Starts.

In addition to these promising strategies to reduce re-offending by youth who have already committed crimes, social scientists have also developed an impressive repertoire of intervention techniques in recent years to prevent the onset of delinquency.

Early Childhood Programs. Of all the strategies ever tested to prevent delinquency, the most powerful are those aimed at children in the first four years of life. In Syracuse, New York, the **Family Development Research Program** targeted 108 low-income families, providing home visits (beginning during pregnancy) and quality child care (throughout the pre-school years). When these children were 13 to 16 years old, only 1.5 percent of them had probation records, compared with 17 percent of youth from a control group not receiving the services.[45] None of the targeted youth was a chronic offender, compared with nine percent of the control group. Careful studies in Houston; New Haven; Elmira, NY; and Memphis have also found significant and positive long-term impacts on behavior from intensive home visitation programs in early childhood. **The Perry Preschool Program** in Ypsilanti, Michigan demonstrated that intensive and high-quality early childhood education programs can also be a powerful tool in the prevention of delinquency. The program, which combined high-quality early childhood instruction (taught by masters-level teachers) with parenting assistance and weekly home visits, dramatically reduced the arrest rates during adolescence and young adulthood: by age 27, only seven percent of Perry youth had been arrested five or more times, compared with 35 percent of youth in a randomly-assigned control group.[46]

Treating Conduct Disorders. Children who demonstrate conduct problems early in life are a potential key to defeating the crime problem. Not all problematic children become criminals, of course. Most don't. But the vast majority of youth who do become chronic serious offenders display behavioral problems during childhood. Identifying those children at risk for future delinquency and responding effectively with targeted treatment interventions, therefore, could dramatically reduce the number of chronic criminals in our society.

Several parent training strategies have demonstrated success in the past two decades helping parents resolve the behavior problems of troubled children. For instance, **"The Incredible Years"** parent training program shows parents videotapes that teach positive and appropriate parenting practices and often involves them in group discussions. In one scientific trial, the program resulted in 67 percent to 78 percent of disturbed three to eight year-old children returning to a normal range of behavior after 10-12 weeks of treatment, and these gains remained in place one year after treatment for two-thirds of the children. Another parent management training strategy has demonstrated positive impacts that remained for 10-14 years after treatment. Other prevention programs focus treatment on conduct-disordered children themselves, providing cognitive and behavioral skills training to build children's capacity to control impulses, think through problems, empathize with others, and develop positive solutions to problem situations.

Syracuse Family Development Research Program

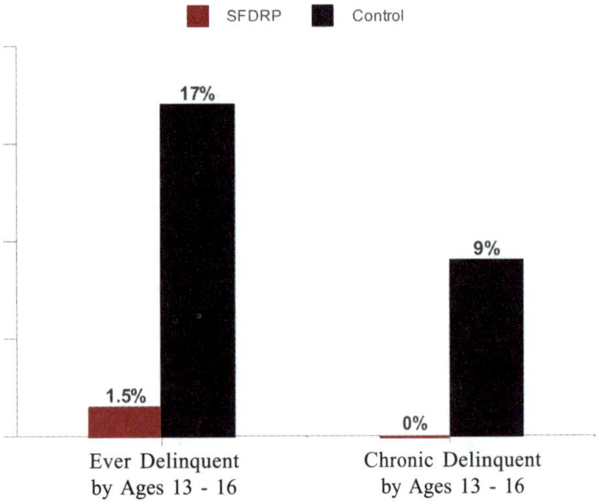

Source: Lally, J.R., Mangione, P.L., & Honig, A.S., "The Syracuse Family Development Research Program: Long-Range Impact of an Early Intervention With Low-Income Children and Their Families," in *Parent Education as Early Childhood Intervention: Emerging Directions in Theory, Research and Practice*, D.R. Powell (Ed.) (Norwood, NJ: Ablex Publishing Corp., 1988).

The most powerful interventions have combined both parent training and social competence development. For instance, a recent trial by Carolyn Webster-Stratton at the University of Washington found that one year after treatment 60 percent and 74 percent of behaviorally disturbed children in families receiving parent training only and child-focused training only achieved a 30 percent or greater reduction in deviant behavior. By contrast, 95 percent of children in families receiving combined parent and child treatment achieved a 30 percent or greater improvement. **The Montreal Longitudinal Experimental Study** also combined parent training with cognitive behavioral skills training to great success, targeting 166 French Canadian boys with disruptive behavior problems. At the end of the two-year program, no significant behavior differences emerged between participating children and those in a control group. Two years later (ages 11-12), however, participating youths engaged in fewer fights, were half as likely to suffer serious school adjustment problems, and were far less likely to be involved in delinquent activities than children in the control group. By early adolescence, the participating children were far less likely to join a gang or to abuse alcohol or drugs.[47]

The most powerful interventions [for behaviorally disturbed children] have combined both parent training and social competence development. For instance, a recent trial by Carolyn Webster-Stratton at the University of Washington found that . . . 95 percent of children in families receiving combined parent and child treatment achieved a 30 percent or greater improvement.

School-Based Prevention. Few of the violence, delinquency, and substance abuse prevention efforts being undertaken in schools today have been subject to meaningful outcome evaluation. The evidence that is available indicates that most prevention programs currently offered by schools – particularly quick, one-dimensional programs implemented without strong planning or staff training – make little or no long-term difference on youth behavior. This lack of impact by school-based prevention programs is not due to a shortage of effective program models. ***Prevention researchers consistently find that school-based programs can produce sustained behavior changes when they are carefully implemented, developmentally appropriate, sustained over time and focused at least in part on building social competence.*** Several school-based prevention strategies have demonstrated the power to reduce either delinquency or known precursors to delinquency such as substance abuse and anti-social behavior.

A **Bullying Prevention** project pioneered in Norway found that by engaging the entire school community (students, teachers, and parents), setting and enforcing clear rules about bullying behavior, and supporting and protecting the victims of bullying, the incidence of bullying was cut in half. Rates of vandalism, truancy, and theft in participating schools declined as well. The project has been replicated in Germany, England, and South Carolina, and has substantially reduced bullying in every case.[48] The **Good Behavior Game**, a Grades One and Two curriculum to help children better adapt to the school environment generally and to curb aggressive behavior, has led to improved behavior among all students in targeted classrooms during the program period, and yielded lasting gains among boys who were highly aggressive when they entered first grade. Apparently, participation in the Good Behavior Game shifts boys who are initially aggressive onto a different and more pro-social life trajectory.[49]

The **Resolving Conflicts Creatively** and **Peacebuilders** programs also aim to alter the school climate. Resolving Conflicts Creatively, which operates in at least 350 schools nationwide, provides conflict resolution training for teachers, administrators, and parents along with classroom instruction for students and peer mediation to resolve disputes between students. A comprehensive 1999 evaluation found that students in classrooms where teachers taught many RCC lessons (average of 25 per year) showed far less aggressive behavior (and also better academic achievement) than children who were not exposed to the program.[50] Peacebuilders, which operates in some 400 schools in Arizona, California, Utah, and Ohio, does not offer a classroom curriculum but instead focuses on improving the school climate by teaching and reinforcing five simple principles school-wide: (1) praise people, (2) avoid put-downs, (3) seek wise people as advisers and friends, (4) notice and correct the hurts they cause, and (5) right wrongs. Peacebuilders is currently in the midst of a six-year federal evaluation and preliminary findings show teacher-rated increases in social competence and declines in aggressive behavior. Participating schools have also experienced reductions in student visits to the nurse's office for treatment of injuries compared to control schools.[51]

A multi-component **Social Development Program** in Seattle offered school children six years (grades 1-6) of social competence training, parenting skills training, and training for teachers in classroom management and interactive instructional techniques. Researchers followed the students to age 18 and found that, compared with a control group, they committed fewer violent delinquent acts, did less heavy drinking, were less likely to have multiple sexual partners, misbehaved less in school and were more committed and attached to school.[52]

Positive Youth Development. Because delinquency prevention has not typically been the primary goal of after-school activities and other positive youth development programs, few studies have measured their direct impact on delinquency and crime. Yet logic suggests their potential to significantly curb delinquent activity. The peak hours for juvenile crime and delinquency come on weekdays between 2 pm and 8 pm. Four recent studies illustrate the power of positive youth development programs to limit delinquency.

- In Ottawa, Canada, an after-school recreation program targeting all children in a local public housing project led to a 75 percent drop in the number of arrests for youth residing in the targeted project, while the arrest rate for youth in a nearby housing project not benefitting from the programs rose by 67 percent.[53]

- A 1991 Columbia University study compared public housing complexes with and without an on-site Boys & Girls club. Complexes with a club that also delivered a social skills training curriculum for youth suffered significantly less vandalism, drug trafficking, and juvenile crime.[54]

- A 1996 study of the Big Brothers/Big Sisters mentoring project revealed that youth assigned a mentor were 46 percent less likely to take drugs, 27 percent less likely to drink alcohol, and almost one-third less likely to strike another person than a control group of youth who applied but were placed on a waiting list.[55]

- In a 1994 study of the Quantum Opportunities Program (QOP), high-risk youth who participated in an intensive four-year after-school program of career preparation, life skills training, and academic enrichment proved far more likely than a randomly assigned control group to graduate high school, attend college, and delay parenting. QOP participants were convicted of less than one-sixth as many crimes as control group youth (.04 convictions per QOP participant vs. .26 convictions per control youth).[56]

In addition, "service-learning" initiatives – in which students' academic lessons are derived from community service work activities – have reduced arrests, violence, and other behavior problems, according to several published studies. In its publications *Some Things DO Make a Difference* and *MORE Things That DO Make a Difference*, the American Youth Policy Forum has identified dozens of youth development programs with proven results – including several like YouthBuild and the National Guard ChalleNGe Program that target delinquent youth and other youth at high risk for delinquency.

Mounting Comprehensive Community Strategies.

Each of the strategies detailed in this chapter can help to reduce juvenile offending. These specific program and policy reform models provide only a starting point for local efforts to reduce juvenile crime, however. The complex problems of delinquency and youth violence do not lend themselves to one-size-fits-all solutions. Each community faces different challenges, and each possesses a different mix of assets for combatting delinquency.

The cities, counties and communities that are proving most successful in reducing juvenile crime rates are those that have focused comprehensively and engage key leaders from multiple sectors. Only when a broad-based group of community leaders examines the specific trends, problems, assets, and risk factors affecting their youth can localities target their limited resources for juvenile justice and delinquency prevention effectively. Only when a broad array of leaders becomes informed and active in addressing delinquency issues comprehensively can resistance to reform be overcome. More and more, crime experts acknowledge that developing a holistic, integrated crime reduction plan is a critical step for any locality seeking significant and sustained progress against youth crime.

Learning from Boston. After experiencing a steep rise in juvenile and young adult violence in the late 1980s, Boston suffered 152 homicides in 1990 – up from less than 100 per year throughout most of the 1980s. The major source of this violence was youth gangs, whose struggle for control of territory in crack distribution led to a substantial increase in the numbers of youth acquiring and carrying guns, which in turn spilled over into additional shootings unrelated to drugs. In 1998, eight years later, Boston suffered just 35 murders — down 78 percent from the 1990 level and equaling the City's lowest rate since the mid-1960s. During a 29-month period (from the summer of 1995 through December 1997), not a single juvenile gun homicide was committed in Boston.[57]

What turned youth crime in Boston around? The answer can be found in Boston's comprehensive approach – intensive research and planning by leaders in various sectors, followed by an aggressive, coordinated and customized anti-violence campaign.

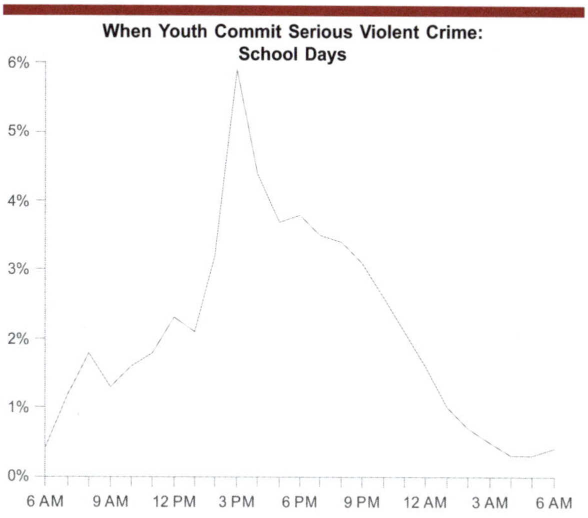

Source: National Center for Juvenile Justice

Some elements of this campaign focused on law enforcement. Boston's police department convened a **Youth Violence Strike Force** with 45 full-time police officers and 15 officials from other agencies. The Strike Force concentrated on the highest crime neighborhoods in the city and maintained a database on gang leaders and dangerous ex-offenders in the community. The **Boston Gun Project** – jointly initiated by the Strike Force and the federal Bureau of Alcohol, Tobacco and Firearms – concentrated investigators' attention not just on specific crimes but also the guns used in the crimes, aggressively tracing the source of guns used in crimes and prosecuting those involved in illegal gun trafficking. In 1994, law enforcement officials began **Operation Cease Fire**, a "zero tolerance" policy for gun violence. Police began vigorously enforcing gun laws against any gang member caught carrying guns or committing violent gun crimes, and then turned over those caught for federal prosecution — which can carry far greater penalties then local statutes.

In addition, Boston also strengthened efforts both in its juvenile justice system and in delinquency prevention. Historically, Boston's probation officers and police department did not work well together. Police personnel often criticized probation officers for doing too little to supervise dangerous offenders — many of whom were still deeply involved in gangs and other criminal activities. Yet probation officers have several privileges that police don't, including the right to search probationers' homes and arrest them without a warrant. Based on a suggestion from a veteran Boston probation officer, police and probation officers have been working together since 1992 on a project called **Operation Night Light**. Police and probation officers conduct joint evening patrols, making nighttime visits to the homes of high-risk probationers. Those out after curfew receive warnings at first, but repeated violations result in a return to court and sometimes to jail.[58] In addition, Boston has created an **Alternatives to Incarceration Network** to offer community-based supervision and positive support for less dangerous youth who would otherwise be confined in a detention center or prison.

The final key element in the Boston strategy has been outreach and support for youth. City-funded "streetworkers" and counselors from local youth agencies have worked hand in hand with law enforcement officials to send youth the clear message that gunplay will no longer be tolerated. Meanwhile, Boston's youth violence strategy also relied on positive youth activities provided by community agencies like the **Ella J. Baker House**, a drop-in center for youth in the North Dorchester neighborhood and the hub of an extensive array of youth outreach and programming. In fact, the Baker House is just one of many youth resources offered through the **Boston Ten Point Coalition** – a citywide confederation of congregations that have dedicated themselves to serving young people while helping authorities combat juvenile crime. Meanwhile, Boston has created a **Youth Service Providers Network** to work with youth referred by police in three of the City's most troubled neighborhoods.

Not only in Boston, but also in Jacksonville, Florida, San Diego, California, Allegheny County (Pittsburgh), PA, and dozens of other jurisdictions throughout the country, community leaders are proving that the most successful approaches for reducing youth crime require community-wide involvement and multi-pronged action. "Several cities in the United States have distinguished themselves in the fight to reduce crime over the past decade," wrote the National Crime Prevention Council in 1999. "Cities on the crest of the crime reduction wave have demonstrated a capacity to fuse grass-roots support, political and bureaucratic will, and crime prevention best practices into a distinct and changed way of doing business."[59]

A Giant Step Forward? Taken together, advances in theory and practice in juvenile crime prevention offer America the opportunity to take a giant step forward in our fight to control adolescent crime. Unfortunately, most citizens in our nation – and most policymakers as well – remain unaware of the potential for progress. Funding for replication of model programs and for policy reforms based on research-proven principles are moving at a snail's pace – shoved aside by popular but misguided ideas, and unable to penetrate resistant juvenile justice and delinquency prevention systems.

Part Two: BARRIERS

(Why America Could Miss Our Best Chance to Control Youth Crime)

Throughout the 1980s and 1990s, empirical knowledge of what works in juvenile crime prevention expanded greatly. National, state and local leaders paid little notice.

Affordable intervention strategies with the potential to revolutionize juvenile justice and delinquency prevention remained quietly on the sidelines as noisy battles over juvenile crime were being fought throughout the nation. Clear lessons about what works and doesn't work in preventing delinquency and reversing delinquent behavior patterns went and still go unheard and unheeded.

Why is the message not getting through? Why do we as a nation foresake treasures of knowledge on an issue so alarming to the vast body of the American public. The following pages explore two reasons, two powerful but misguided ideas that co-opted most of the attention in the juvenile crime debates of the 1990s and drowned out the calm voices of science and reason.

Chapter Two

SUPERPREDATORS OR SCAPEGOATS?

(How Severe is America's Juvenile Crime Problem?)

During the 1990s, America's youth set an all-time record in one telling crime category. No, not school violence. Not drug dealing or delinquency, either. Rather, the all-time record was in negative media attention.

Consider the weekly news magazines. Even before the Columbine killings in 1999, *Time* magazine devoted three cover stories to youth crime in the 1990s with titles including "Children Without Pity," "The Deadly Love Affair Between Kids and Their Guns," and "Teenage Time Bomb." *Newsweek* devoted at least two cover stories to youth violence, as did *U.S. News and World Report*. Even the usually upbeat *People Magazine* joined the chorus in 1997, with a cover story entitled "Heartbreaking Crimes: Kids Without a Conscience."

Such hard-edged, high-profile coverage of youth crime was not limited to news magazines. A survey of newspaper coverage in St. Louis found that the *St. Louis Post-Dispatch* devoted twice as much coverage to teenage crime as it did to positive coverage of youth, and the survey's author concluded that "most daily newspapers portray teenagers negatively."[60] Likewise, more than half (55 percent) of all local television news stories involving youth focus on violent crime, a study in California found, and more than two-thirds (68 percent) of all stories about violence involve young people.[61] Overall, crime jumped from sixth place among all issues on national TV news shows in 1991 to first place in 1993, 1994, 1995, and 1997 – taking a step back to number two in 1996 only to make room for that year's presidential election.[62]

Perhaps the most remarkable facet of this explosion in crime coverage was that it did not correspond with rising crime rates. ***The rates of violent crime, property crime, and overall index crimes in the United States have decreased every year since 1991, just as the media coverage of crime***

mushroomed. The rates of youth crime have also declined every year since 1993, after rising significantly in the early part of the decade (as well as in the late 1980s).

The epidemic of media crime coverage was unrelated to the actual incidence of crime. Nonetheless, it exerted a powerful influence on the juvenile crime debate during the 1990s, and it remains today the pivotal ingredient in the public's understanding of crime issues. Sixty-five percent of Americans say their feelings about crime are based mainly on what they see in the media, while only 21 percent base their judgements on personal experience.[63] In other words, observed crime commentator Peter Elikann, "the media (our modern-day version of the ancient trumpeter), decides how our entire culture will look at and then act against crime."[64]

When the Gallup organization conducted a poll in 1994, a nationwide sample of adults believed that juveniles were responsible for 43 percent of all violent crime – more than three times the percentage of violent crime actually committed by kids 17-and-under in 1994 (14 percent) and more than 4 times the percentage of murders committed by youth (10 percent). Americans hold "a greatly inflated view of the amount of crime committed by people under the age of 18," Gallup concluded, attributing the misperception to "news coverage of violent crime committed by juveniles."[65]

Despite the substantial decline in adolescent crime since 1993, two-thirds of the public believe that adolescent crime is still rising, reported Vincent Schiraldi, director of the Justice Policy Institute in November 1999.[66] In Florida, a 1998 poll found that 89 percent of adults believed that teens are becoming more violent.[67] This continuing public concern over juvenile crime can be traced largely to the series of calamitous school shootings that began in Pearl, Mississippi in October 1997 and culminated in Columbine, Colorado in April 1999. Following intense, vivid, ubiquitous coverage of the first school shooting incidents, 71 percent of adults responding to a May 1998 *Wall Street Journal* poll believed that a killing was likely in their local schools. In November 1999, two-thirds of adults in a *Washington Post* poll listed school violence as something that is "worrying me the most these days."[68] ***In reality, school violence has declined in recent years and remains extremely rare. In a nation with roughly 50 million school children, only 26 people died in school violence during the 1998-99 school year – far fewer than the number of Americans (88) who were killed by lightning in 1996.***[69]

Beyond the Myth of the Superpredator.

Public fears about youth crime have also been heightened in recent years due to dire warnings issued by a handful of criminologists in 1995. These scholars theorized that a dangerous new breed of juvenile "superpredators" was emerging in America, and they predicted that a "ticking time bomb" of youth crime would erupt early in the new century due to a substantial projected increase in the size of the nation's youth population. These alarming predictions captured enormous attention from the media, including cover stories in both *Time* magazine and *U.S. News & World Report.* Rhetoric about superpredators and ticking time bombs quickly found its way into the speeches of public officials from both political parties. Yet these predictions were flawed in four regards:

Juvenile crime is not getting worse. In the decade before the superpredator predictions first appeared, youth crime had risen rapidly. From 1984 to 1994, the number of murders committed by youth increased three-fold, from 823 to 2,320. The overall serious violent crime rate (including homicide, rape, robbery and aggravated assault) among youth ages 12-17 also rose rapidly – from 29 offenses per 1,000 youth in 1986 to almost 52 in 1993. But then, as quickly as they had begun rising (but with a lot less fanfare), juvenile crime

Juvenile Violent Crime Rates, 1993 and 1998

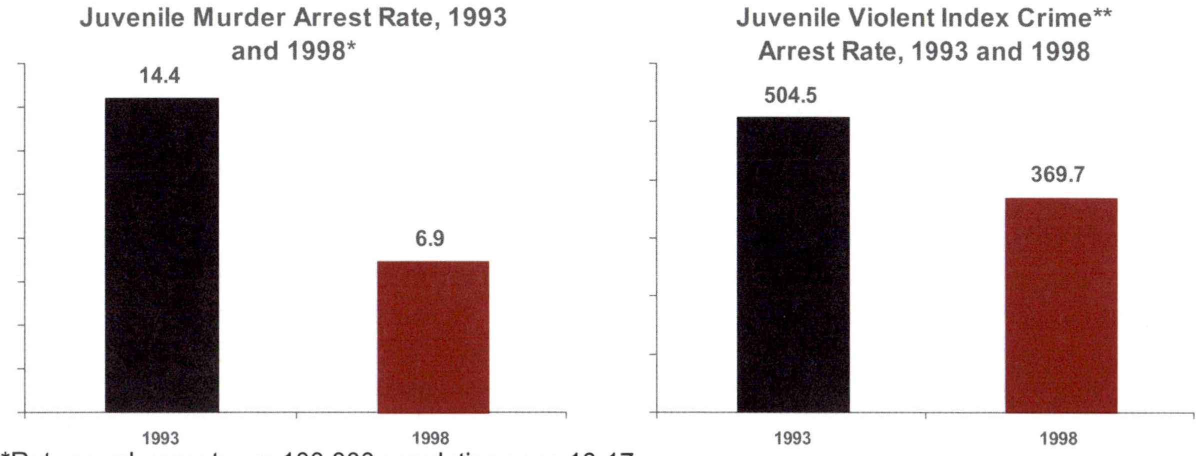

*Rate equals arrests per 100,000 population ages 10-17

**Violent Index Crimes include murder, rape, armed robbery, and aggravated assault.

rates started to fall. The juvenile homicide rate inched down three percent in 1994, then another 19 percent in 1995 and 17 percent more in 1996. ***By 1998, the latest year for which data are now available, the juvenile homicide rate had declined by a remarkable 52 percent from its 1993 high – bringing the youth murder rate to its lowest level since 1987.*** The combined rates for all serious violent offenses (murder, rape, robbery, and aggravated assault) declined 32 percent for youth ages 15-17 from 1994-98 and 27 percent for children 14 and under.

Violent Crime Index Arrests of Juveniles Ages 10-12, Percent of all Juvenile Arrests

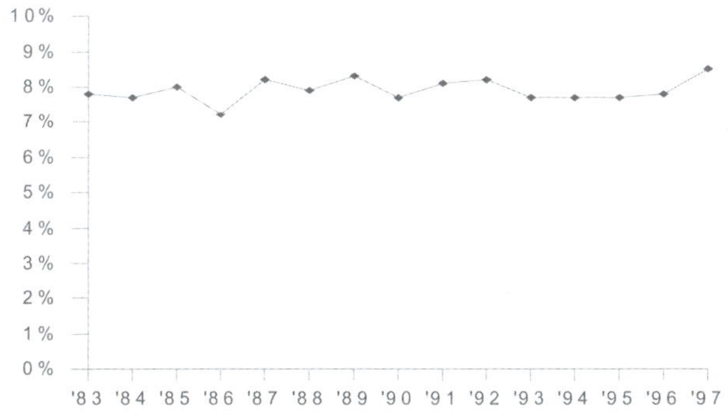

Source: Analysis of arrest data from unpublished FBI reports for 1980 through 1994 and the FBI's *Crime in the United States* reports for 1995, 1996 and 1997 and population data from the Bureau of the Census for 1980 through 1989 from *Current Population Reports,* p.25-1095, and for 1990 through 1997 from *Estimates of the Population of States by Age, Sex, Race, and Hispanic Origin: 1990-1997.* This chart is available online at: http://www.ncjrs.org/html/ojjdp/nationalreport99/chapter5.pdf

Juvenile crime is not getting younger. Another tenet of the superpredator theory (and a main staple of media coverage in recent years) holds that very young offenders are committing more and more serious crime. Despite the sensational coverage lavished on a handful of high-profile cases, however, the actual incidence of crimes by very young offenders has almost exactly paralleled that of older youth. For property crimes, the arrest rate of 10-12 year-old offenders in 1997 was eight percent lower than in 1980, and 10-12 year-olds represented the same percentage of total juvenile arrests (13 percent) in 1980 and 1997. For violent crimes, ***10-12 year-olds' percentage of all juvenile violent crime arrests has remained at or near eight percent for 15 consecutive years. While very young offenders often receive intense media attention, they account for only a small (and stable) percentage of juvenile arrests.***

The projected rise in the youth population over the coming two decades does not doom America to increasing juvenile crime. The "ticking time bomb" hypothesis was based on the notion that increases in the size of the adolescent population inevitably lead to a rise in youth crime. In fact, the correlation between youth population and youth crime has not been strong in recent decades. "History shows that it's a fool's errand to try to predict future crime trends," wrote the National Center for Juvenile Justice (NCJJ) in 1999, four years after itself making the mistake of forecasting a substantial rise in juvenile crime during the late 1990s and early 2000s. "Changes in juvenile crime arrests are not closely tied to changes in the juvenile population," NCJJ concluded. "No one has been able to predict juvenile violence trends accurately."[70]

Succeeding generations are not becoming more prone to violence. The central tenet of the superpredator theory was that the current and future generation of young people will prove more dangerous and less law-abiding than earlier generations – that each new cohort of youngsters will offend more frequently and more violently than the last. When criminologists Phillip Cook and John Laub analyzed the juvenile murder rates of minority males in 1998, however, they found no evidence for this trend.[71] Cook and Laub reported that the cohort of minority youth who were ages 15-19 in 1990 committed murders at an alarming rate that year. But in 1985 these same youth committed homicides at the lowest rate of any cohort of 10-14 year-olds since the 1960s. Likewise, the same 20-24 year olds who demonstrated high murder rates in 1990 had shown low murder rates as teens in 1985. In other words, the juvenile crime wave of the late 1980s and early 1990s was not the product of a deviant new generation of adolescents, but a temporary outbreak of violence that cut across the age spectrum of youth and young adults – and then subsided. "There is no steady downhill progression where each cohort is more deadly than the last," Cook and Laub concluded.[72]

The juvenile crime wave of the late 1980s and early 1990s was not the product of a deviant new generation of adolescents, but a temporary outbreak of violence that cut across the age spectrum of youth and young adults – and then subsided. "There is no steady downhill progression where each cohort is more deadly than the last."

Epidemiology of an Outbreak.

What caused the decade-long outbreak of violent behavior among youth and young adults in the late 1980s and early 1990s? Criminologists have not found a single cause to explain this violence epidemic. Instead, most experts point to a combination of factors:

- *The introduction of crack cocaine in the mid-1980s*, which created an enormous market and precipitated a free-for-all among drug traffickers – perhaps the bloodiest turf wars ever seen in the illicit drug industry. Throughout the nation, tens of thousands of young people were recruited to participate in crack distribution – where guns and violence became an integral fact of everyday life.

- *The proliferation of guns.* Particularly in neighborhoods where the crack wars waged, gun carrying became the habit of an alarming number of young people. The number of young people arrested for weapons possession nearly doubled from 1988 to 1993, and surveys found an alarming percentage of youth either carried guns on a routine basis or had easy access to them. As a result, the number of juvenile fire-arm homicides quadrupled from 1984 to 1994, while juvenile homicides not involving fire-arms have held constant for twenty years.

- *The rapid rise in gang membership.* Once an urban phenomenon concentrated primarily in large cities, gangs have spread to cities and towns throughout the nation. From 1991 to 1993, the estimated number of gangs nationwide increased 77 percent (to 8,625 gangs) and the number of gang members increased 52 percent (to 378,087 gang members). In 1995, the National Youth Gang Center identified 23,000 gangs in some 2,000 cities and towns with membership of 665,000 gang members.[73] This growth trend in gangs had severe implications for juvenile crime, because youth who belong to gangs commit substantially more and more serious crimes than high-risk youth who are not gang-involved. In Rochester, New York, gang members comprised only one-third of delinquent youth sampled in a recent study, but they committed 69 percent of the violent crimes, 68 percent of the property crimes, and 70 percent of the drug crimes in the entire sample.[74]

Criminologists hypothesize that the combination of all these factors created the conditions for a violence epidemic in the late 1980s and early '90s. Borrowing from the language of public health experts, they surmise that neighborhood conditions reached a "tipping point" at which crime escalated out of control. Violence begat violence. As they entered the crack market many young people armed themselves for protection and competitive advantage. Soon youth not involved in the drug trade felt compelled to arm themselves as well. Fear of being victimized led many to strike first, and a brutal "code of the streets" emerged, in the words of University of Pennsylvania sociologist Elijah Anderson, where safety, status, and even survival were predicated on a youth's willingness and capacity to take violent action.[75]

"I think we better reconsider the superpredator theory, because it just didn't work. The prophets of gloom and doom have been proven wrong."

As the '90s wore on and crack markets settled, the situation calmed. Gun carrying and gun arrests dwindled (though not yet to their pre-1988 levels), communities organized against crime, law enforcement agencies developed new tactics to target gangs and gun crime, and violence began to ebb. Gradually, and without fanfare, the epidemic subsided. Youth crime rates returned to levels consistent with earlier generations, and the myth of the superpredator was laid bare.

"I think we better reconsider the superpredator theory, because it just didn't work," Jack Levin, the director of Northeastern University's Brudnick Center on Violence, told a reporter in 1999. "The prophets of gloom and doom have been proven wrong."[76]

A Scapegoat Generation?

In retrospect, there is no escaping the conclusion that reporters and public officials rushed to judgement on youth crime and fanned the flame of unwarranted public fears.

"Experts have identified a 1990s demographic scapegoat for America's pandemic violent crime: our own kids," wrote youth scholar Mike Males in 1996. "A mushrooming media scare campaign about the coming 'storm' of 'teenage violence' waged by liberal and conservative politicians and experts alike is in full roar."[77] To help right these false impressions and derail the cycle of ever-increasing fear of youth crime, Males authored a book, *Scapegoat Generation: America's War on Adolescents*.[78]

Juvenile Arrests in 1998

Most Serious Offenses	1998 Estimated Number of Arrests	Percent of Total Juvenile Arrests: Females	Percent of Total Juvenile Arrests: Under Age 15	Percent Change 1989-98	Percent Change 1994-98	Percent Change 1997-98
Total	**2,603,300**	**27%**	**31%**	**24%**	**1%**	**-4%**
Crime Index Total	708,300	26	38	-9	-18	-11
Violent Crime Index	112,200	17	31	15	-19	-8
Murder and nonnegligent manslaughter	2,100	8	9	-23	-48	-12
Forcible rape	5,300	2	37	-3	-9	0
Robbery	32,500	9	25	9	-29	-17
Aggravated assault	72,300	22	33	21	-13	-3
Property Crime Index	596,100	28	39	-12	-17	-11
Burglary	116,100	11	38	-22	-17	-9
Larceny-theft	417,100	35	41	-4	-14	-12
Motor vehicle theft	54,100	17	26	-39	-40	-15
Arson	9,000	11	66	10	-24	-8
Nonindex						
Other assaults	237,700	31	41	68	10	2
Forgery and counterfeiting	7,100	35	13	-2	-16	-12
Fraud	11,300	33	16	44	-8	6
Embezzlement	1,600	42	5	-5	56	19
Stolen Property (buying, receiving, possessing)	33,800	13	26	-27	-27	-12
Vandalism	126,800	12	44	9	-18	-3
Weapons (carrying, possessing, etc.)	45,200	9	32	15	-30	-8
Prostitution and commercialized vice	1,400	50	14	-6	18	4
Sex Offenses (except forcible rape and prostitution)	15,900	7	50	-1	-5	-4
Drug abuse violations	205,800	14	16	86	26	-3
Gambling	1,600	3	14	86	-61	-34
Offenses against the family and children	10,200	7	37	166	103	3
Driving under the influence	21,000	17	3	3	39	13
Liquor law violations	157,300	30	10	20	39	10
Drunkenness	24,600	18	13	2	23	2
Disorderly conduct	183,700	28	35	61	20	-4
Vagrancy	2,900	17	26	-1	-37	-17
All other offenses (except traffic)	453,000	25	27	53	20	4
Suspicion	1,300	24	26	-56	-17	-9
Curfew and loitering	187,800	30	27	178	49	-3
Runaways	165,100	58	40	-5	-21	-15

Source: Juvenile Arrests 1998

In attempting to reverse the momentum (or minimize the impact) of sensational media coverage and tough-on-youth political rhetoric, many youth advocates have sought to downplay the extent of juvenile crime and the risks of a significant juvenile crime increase in the new century. In order to rehabilitate youth in the eyes of adults (and political leaders especially), advocates have frequently invoked the following facts:

- Even at the height of the juvenile crime wave in the early 1990s, only five percent of juveniles ages 10-17 were arrested each year, and less than ten percent of these youth arrests were for violent offenses. Thus, fewer than one-half of one-percent of all youth were charged with a *violent* offense in any year.[79]

- The percentage of property crime nationwide committed by youth has declined substantially over the past 30 years. In the 1960s and early '70s, more than half of all individuals arrested for burglary, larceny-theft, motor vehicle theft, and arson were under 18. Since 1985, however, youths' percentage of property crime arrests has held between 30 and 35 percent every year. Moreover, because young people tend to commit crimes in groups (leading to multiple arrests for a single crime), only 20 percent of property crimes which lead to arrest are committed by persons 17-and-under.[80]

- Even after the rapid surge in juvenile homicides from 1984-94, only 10 percent of homicides cleared by arrest in 1994 were committed by youths.[81] By 1998, that percentage had declined to six percent.[82]

- Youth are far more likely to be victimized by violence than to commit violence: 350,000 juveniles were arrested for violent felonies and misdemeanors in 1993, while parents or caretakers alone committed 370,000 confirmed violent and sexual offenses against children and youth. Among the 1,268 children under 18 who were murdered in 1994 and whose killers' ages were known, 70 percent of the murderers were adults – not other youths. Of the 9,004 adult murder victims in 1994, 91 percent of the killers were adults.[83]

- Most violent crime is concentrated in a small number of major urban centers. Eighty-four percent of all counties nationwide did not suffer a single juvenile homicide in 1995, and fully one-third of all juvenile homicides were committed in just four cities – Chicago, Detroit, Los Angeles, and New York.[84]

In March 2000, the Justice Policy Institute released a study tracing the patterns of youth and adult crime in California from 1978 to 1998. Violent felony rates for youth declined by 40 percent over the two decades, the study found, while felony arrests for adults 30-and-older increased. "Not only were juvenile arrest rates lower in the late 1990s than at any time in the previous 25 years," the authors noted, but "those juveniles who were arrested were being charged with less serious offenses: 38 percent were charged with felonies in 1979 and 33 percent were charged with felonies in 1998."[85]

Even after the rapid surge in juvenile homicides from 1984-94, only 10 percent of homicides cleared by arrest in 1994 were committed by youths. By 1998, that percentage had declined to six percent.

Even Without Superpredators, Concerns About Youth Crime are Real.

Given the scourge of negative media attention showered on young people in the 1990s, and given the public's inflated perceptions of young peoples' contribution to our nation's overall crime problem, it is important to place these countervailing realities before the public eye. Looked at in historical perspective, however, the youth crime rate remains well above historical averages, and youth remains the peak period in life for offending of all types, including violence.

Even setting aside the dramatic spike in youth violence in the late '80s and early '90s, the long-term trend shows a steady upward progression: 377.4 violent crime arrests per 100,000 young people ages 15-17 in 1970; 478.1 violent crimes in

Youth Violent Index Crime Arrest Rates, 1970-1998*

Arrests per 100,000 population

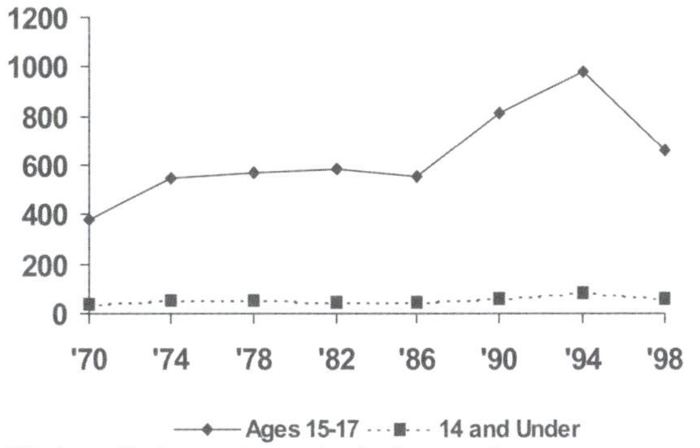

* Violent Index crimes include murder, rape, armed robbery, and aggravated assault.

Source: FBI, Uniform Crime Reports.

Violent Index Crime Arrest Rates By Age Group, 1980 and 1997

Violent Index Crime Arrests per 100,000 Population

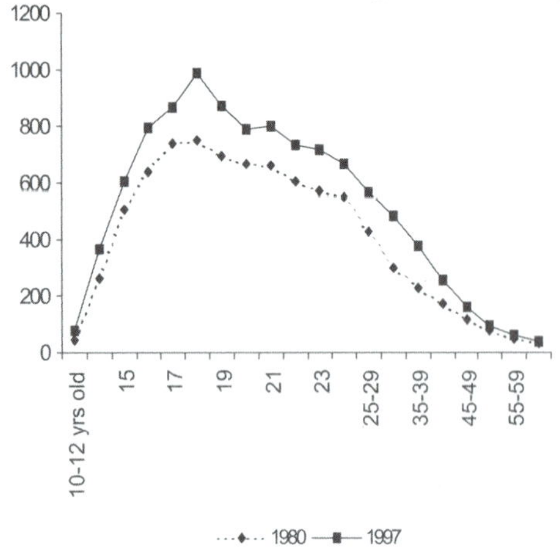

Source: Chart can be found at http://www.ncjrs.org/html/ojjdp/nationalreport99/chapter5.pdf

1974; 571.6 in 1978; 584.0 in 1982; 554.4 crimes in 1986; and then 661.9 per 100,000 youth in 1998 (after large jumps in 1990 and '94).[86] Likewise, from an international perspective America's rate of youth violence – like its rate of adult violence – continues to stand alone. Our firearm-related homicide death rate for children under age 15, for instance, is nearly 16 times the combined of 25 other industrialized countries worldwide.[87]

Also, both from self-reports and official arrest records we know that offending rates climb rapidly beginning in the early teen years, spike at age 18, and then decline steadily thereafter. In 1997, the violent crime arrest rate per 100,000 population was less than 100 for 10 to12-year-olds, 368 for 13 to14-year-olds, 606 for 15-year-olds, 796 for 16-year-olds, 867 for 17-year-olds, and 987 for 18-year-olds. After that, however, the arrest rate declined to 872 for 19-year-olds, to 787 and 799 or so for 20 and 21-year-olds, and to lesser numbers for each successive age cohort throughout the life span. The violent crime arrest rate for 35 to 39-year-olds was roughly the same as for 13 to14-year-olds, and for 50 to 59-year-olds the rate was roughly equivalent to that of 10 to12-year-olds.[88]

Self-report surveys reveal that the majority of youth engage in some form of law-breaking during adolescence, and a substantial fraction take part in serious, repeated and/or violent criminal acts. Looking to the future, many of the factors that tend to heighten delinquency – weak parental supervision, child abuse and neglect, school failure, substance abuse, neighborhood disorganization, youth gangs – remain rampant in our society.

Tending the Garden.

So how serious a problem is juvenile crime in our society? How much need we fear the coming generation? After peeling rhetoric from hard fact, the evidence reveals that the alarming forecasts and hyperbolic commentary so commonplace during the 1990s were irresponsible and misplaced. Juvenile crime is not rising inexorably, violent acts are not being committed by ever-younger children, and our schools are not being overrun by a cadre of lawless and desperate teen

After peeling rhetoric from hard fact, the evidence reveals that the alarming forecasts and hyperbolic commentary so commonplace during the 1990s were irresponsible and misplaced. Juvenile crime is not rising inexorably, violent acts are not being committed by ever-younger children, and our schools are not being overrun by a cadre of lawless and desperate teen menaces. Most important, there is no evidence that the current and coming generation of young people is any less moral or more violence-prone than young people in earlier generations.

menaces. Most important, there is no evidence that the current and coming generation of young people is any less moral or more violence-prone than young people in earlier generations.

These realities, however, should not lull us into complacency. Just like the children of earlier times, the next generation will be at risk for mischief and even menacing crime during their adolescent and young adult years. The number of adolescents and young adults in the peak crime years will climb in the coming decade. While these facts by no means guarantee a renewed crime epidemic, the demographic reality of a rising youth population certainly heightens the risks.

In a 1999 book about violent youth entitled *Lost Boys*, James Garbarino of Cornell University quotes a passage written by Zen master and one-time Nobel Peace Prize nominee Thich Nath Hanh: "When you plant lettuce, if it does not grow well, you don't blame the lettuce. You look into the reasons it is not doing well. It may need fertilizer, or more water, or less sun. You never blame the lettuce."[89] The imperative is clear: we ignore juvenile crime at our peril. We ought not blame the lettuce, but we need to tend the garden.

Chapter Three

RHYME WITHOUT REASON

(Second Thoughts on "Adult Time for Adult Crime")

"Adult time for adult crime." Almost from the moment they entered the political lexicon in the early '90s, these five words, this simple rhyme, began sparking a movement that has reshaped our nation's policy towards adolescent crime in a few short years.

For almost a century, state laws throughout the nation adhered to the notion that children and youth who misbehave and break laws should be subject to a different system of justice than adult criminals – a system focused more on rehabilitation than punishment, more on the needs of troubled youth than on the society's interest in just deserts. Children, because they are less competent and more vulnerable than adults, should not be held as culpable for their wrongdoings. Except in extreme cases, they deserve the chance to mature and reform themselves rather than being branded for life with a criminal record for mistakes made in childhood. Though challenged occasionally, this notion retained pre-eminence throughout most of the century.

Then in the 1990s, the consensus collapsed. "Adult time for adult crime" became a political rallying cry, a guaranteed applause line in any candidate's stump speech. The rhyme also proved a consistent winner in public opinion polls: 80 percent and more of voters in most opinion surveys in the '90s agreed that youthful offenders who commit serious crimes should receive the same punishments as adult wrong-doers.

Suddenly, transfer to criminal court has become common practice in our justice system for youth – not only for a handful of serious offenders, not only for those whose cases have been reviewed in totality by a judge, but for a wide swath of the juvenile offender population.

Legislation followed like an avalanche. In just four years – from 1992 through 1995 – 40 states and the District of Columbia enacted laws to increase the number of young people tried in criminal (i.e., adult) courts, rather than juvenile courts.[90] Again in 1996 and 1997, 25 states changed their statutes regarding jurisdiction of the juvenile courts – and again, virtually all of the new laws aimed to increase the number of youth transferred to criminal court.[91] By the end of the 1997 legislative session, all except six states had enacted or expanded their juvenile transfer laws, and virtually every state allowed offenders as young as 14 to stand trial as adults in at least some circumstances.[92]

Suddenly, transfer to criminal court has become common practice in our justice system for youth – not only for a handful of serious offenders, not only for those whose cases have been reviewed in totality by a judge, but for a wide swath of the juvenile offender population. "Historically, transfer was used sparingly because it was assumed that exposing juveniles to processing and punishment in the criminal courts might do them serious harm," wrote criminologists Donna Bishop and Charles Frazier in 1999. "[More recently], transfer criteria have become inclusive of a broad range of offenders who are neither particularly serious nor particularly chronic... Such policies are consistent with either of two conclusions. In their zeal for retribution, policymakers are willing to ignore the jeopardy into which large numbers of adolescents are placed, or they trust that criminal punishment will ultimately prove beneficial to juvenile offenders and to society.

"In either case," Bishop and Frazier concluded, "we must be concerned about consequences."[93]

Weighing the Consequences.

What does transferring juvenile offenders to criminal court accomplish? Tougher punishment, say supporters, stiff consequences that will turn around youthful offenders and deter youth from committing crimes in the first place. That is the rhetoric, but the grim reality is that widespread use of transfers accomplishes none of these goals. In fact, it actually worsens youth crime, wastes scarce tax dollars, and imposes substantial collateral damage on youth, communities, and the justice system itself. Here's why:

Transfer does not ensure tougher punishment. Historically, juvenile courts have been limited in the severity of sanctions they can impose on youthful offenders – with courts in most states required to set juvenile offenders free by the time they reach their 18th or 21st birthdays. Criminal courts face no such limits. In practice, however, criminal courts do not impose any sterner sanctions than juvenile courts on most youthful offenders. In Florida, for instance, which transfers more youth than any other state in the nation, only 15 percent of transferred juvenile offenders in 1998 were sentenced to prison, and only 34 percent were sentenced to time behind bars in any correctional facility.[94]

"Does the public get more punishment for its money when juveniles are tried as adults?," asked the Urban Institute's Jeffrey Butts and Adele Harrell in 1998. "The use of transfer does increase the *certainty* and *severity* of legal sanctions," they concluded, "but only for the most serious cases, perhaps 30 percent of transferred juveniles." In roughly half the cases transferred, youth receive sentences comparable to those they might have earned in juvenile court, Butts and Harrell reported, while in 20 percent of cases transferred youth are treated more leniently than they would have in juvenile court.[95]

The case of three North Carolina youths support this conclusion. In March 1995, Aurelius, a 15-year-old, was charged with the gang-rape of a 14-year-old girl in his high school auditorium along with two friends. Aurelius was quickly processed in juvenile court and served 18 months in a state training school where he received intensive sex offender treatment. His friends, 16 and 17 at the time of the offense, were transferred to criminal court. One was never convicted of the crime and was later charged with a new assault charge, and the other was not convicted until more than a year after the crime and was then sentenced to only a six-month jail sentence.[96] Overall in North Carolina, only 28 percent of transferred youth receive prison time.[97]

Transfer to adult court increases the criminality of youthful offenders. In study after study, juvenile offenders who are transferred to criminal court recidivate more often, more quickly, and with more serious offenses than those who are retained under juvenile jurisdiction.

- Pennsylvania rewrote its transfer laws in 1996 to mandate transfers for offenders ages 15 and older accused of crimes involving deadly weapons. Two years earlier, however, youth arrested for these crimes who were transferred to criminal court "were more likely to be rearrested – and rearrested more quickly – for new offenses" following release than were youth accused of the same

". . . rather than waiving as many youths as possible to adult court (or ending the juvenile court jurisdiction altogether), it seems much more practical and beneficial to ensure that most youthful offenders are treated as juveniles and direct our attention toward improving the services provided for them."

crimes who were retained in juvenile court, a 1999 study found. "It seems then, that legislative waiver laws (such as the one recently enacted in Pennsylvania) can realistically be expected to have little or no deterrent utility," concluded the author of the Pennsylvania study. "In fact, the evidence actually suggests a 'brutalization effect,' or that these laws may serve to increase the frequency and seriousness of future offending by those youth who are excluded from juvenile court... Therefore, rather than waiving as many youths as possible to adult court (or ending the juvenile court jurisdiction altogether), it seems much more practical and beneficial to ensure that most youthful offenders are treated as juveniles and direct our attention toward improving the services provided for them."[98]

- Likewise in Florida, a study of more than 2,700 matched pairs of transferred and non-transferred offenders found that those who were transferred had a higher re-arrest rate (30 percent vs. 19 percent), shorter period to re-arrest (135 days vs. 227 days), and greater likelihood to be charged with a serious crime (93 percent vs. 85 percent) than those retained in the juvenile justice system.[99]

- A Columbia University study examined two randomly selected groups of youthful offenders (burglars and robbers) arrested in 1981-82 – one group from a two-county area in New York State (where the upper age of juvenile court jurisdiction is 15) and the other group from a similar two-county area in neighboring New Jersey (where the juvenile court's upper age is 17). Among youth arrested on robbery charges, the New York group (tried in criminal court) had significantly higher recidivism than the New Jersey group (mostly retained in juvenile courts): the New York youth had a higher rate of re-arrest (76 percent vs. 67 percent) over four years; were re-arrested more often (2.85 arrests vs. 1.67); and were far more likely to be re-incarcerated (56 percent vs. 41 percent) than the New Jersey youth.[100]

- An analysis of youths in Hennepin County, Minnesota whom prosecutors recommended for waivers to criminal court between 1986 and 1993 found that 58 percent of youths whom judges waived to criminal court committed an additional crime within two years, compared to just 42 percent of the youth retained in juvenile court. "If legislators and courts intend to deter

Juvenile Justice Versus Transfers to Adult Criminal Court: Future Offending by Youthful Offenders in Florida

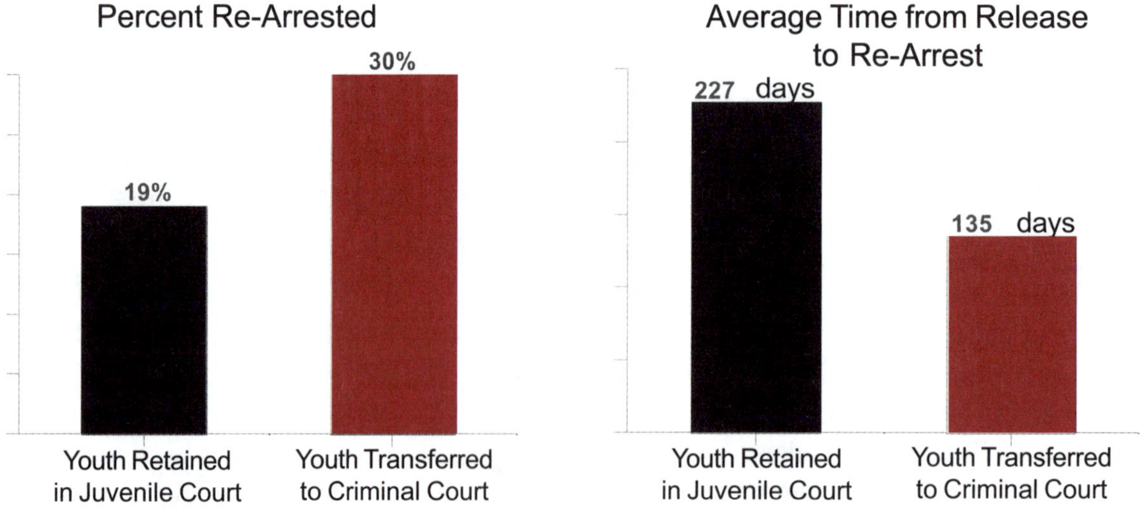

Source: Bishop, D., & Frazier, C., "Consequences of Waiver," in Fagen, J., & Zimring, F.E. (Eds.) *The Changing Borders of Juvenile Justice: Transfer of Adolescents to Criminal Court* (Chicago, IL: University of Chicago Press, forthcoming).

youths from committing additional offenses by subjecting those who persist in delinquency to the more severe punishment of the criminal justice system," the study's authors reported, "our data indicate that they are not achieving that goal."[101]

The threat of adult punishment does not deter youth from crime. In the late 1970s, New York State changed its waiver law to lower the age at which youth accused of murder (age 13) and other violent offenses (age 14) could be transferred to criminal court. Despite an aggressive advertising campaign by authorities in New York to warn youth of the new consequences, violent crime rates among New York youth in the targeted age groups did not decline in comparison with youth in Philadelphia – which had no such transfer law.[102] When Idaho passed a new law in 1981 requiring transfer for all violent youthful offenders ages 14-and-above, the state's juvenile violent crime rate increased, but it decreased in both Montana and Wyoming where the juvenile courts retained jurisdiction of most violent juvenile offenders.[103]

Collateral Damage.

Transferring large numbers of youthful offenders to criminal courts does not reduce the criminality of youth. Worse yet, transfer is also – to borrow a military analogy – inflicting a substantial amount of "collateral damage" on youth, families, and communities throughout our nation.

Confining youthful offenders with adults is dangerous and counterproductive. While some states segregate youthful offenders convicted in criminal court away from adult convicts, or hold them in juvenile institutions until age 18, the population of youth in adult state prisons more than doubled in recent years from 3,400 in 1985 to 7,400 in 1997.[104] Likewise, the number of youth in local jails jumped from 5,100 to 7,000 between 1994 and 1997, a rise of 37 percent in just three years.[105]

Yet adult prisons are perilous places for youthful offenders. Compared with youth confined in juvenile institutions, youthful offenders housed in adult jails and prisons are eight times more likely to commit suicide,[106] five times more likely to be sexually assaulted,[107] twice as likely to be beaten by staff,[108] and 50 percent more likely to be attacked with a weapon.[109] Not surprisingly, then, youth housed in adult jails and prisons also suffer with elevated rates of anxiety and depression, and they are more likely to be placed into specialized mental health treatment units than adult offenders or youth retained under juvenile court supervision.[110]

Compared with youth confined in juvenile institutions, youthful offenders housed in adult jails and prisons are eight times more likely to commit suicide, five times more likely to be sexually assaulted, twice as likely to be beaten by staff, and 50 percent more likely to be attacked with a weapon.

Prisons are, however, a great place for youth to learn the tools of the crime trade from grizzled veterans. In 1998, criminologists Donna Bishop and Charles Frazier surveyed serious youthful offenders in Florida's prisons and juvenile corrections units and found that 55 percent of youth in juvenile corrections expected to remain crime-free after release, while only three percent expected to re-offend. By contrast, only 34 percent of youth serving in adult prisons anticipated that they would stay crime-free, while 18 percent expected to re-offend.[111]

Transfer laws routinely target youth who are not chronic violent or chronic offenders. Prior to passage of Pennsylvania's new transfer law in 1995, 93 percent of youth transferred to criminal court had a prior record of delinquency; after the

Differing Expectations of Florida Juvenile Offenders Incarcerated in Adult Prisons and Juvenile Corrections Facilities

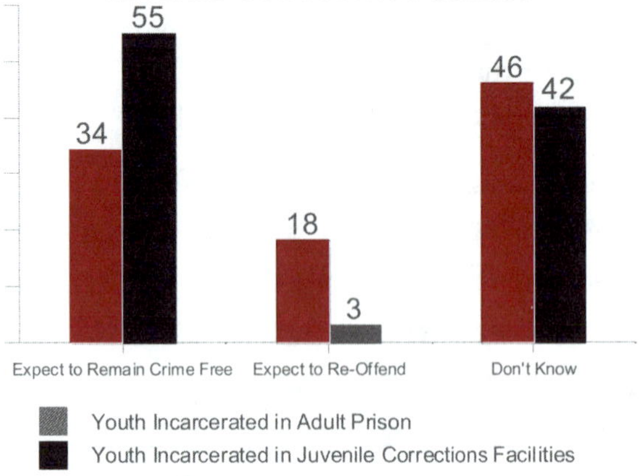

Source: Bishop, D., & Frazier, C., "Consequences of Waiver," in Fagen, J., & Zimring, F.E. (Eds.) *The Changing Borders of Juvenile Justice: Transfer of Adolescents to Criminal Court* (Chicago, IL: University of Chicago Press, forthcoming).

Percentage of Youthful Offenders Transferred to Criminal Courts in Pennsylvania Who Had a Prior Record, Before and After Passage of a Mandatory Transfer Law in 1995

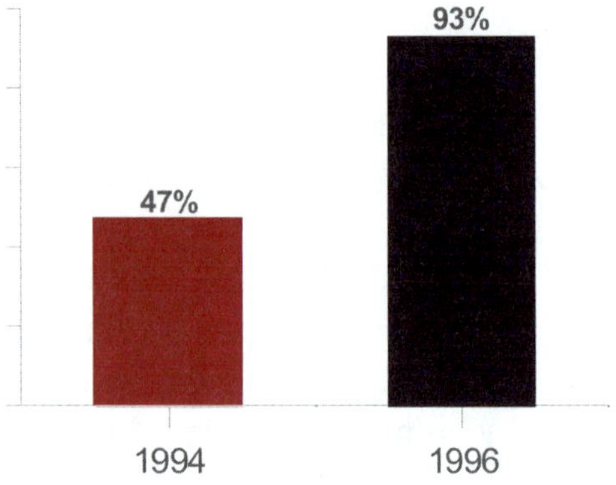

Source: Juvenile Offenders and Victims: 1999 National Report (Pittsburgh, PA: National Center for Juvenile Justice, 1999), pp. 179-180.

new law's passage only 47 percent of transferred youth had a prior record.[112] In South Carolina 72 percent of youthful offenders considered for transfer from 1985-94 had no prior adjudications, yet 82 percent of transfer requests for youth charged with person offenses were granted, along with 46 percent of transfer requests for property offenders with no prior record. In Utah, 82 percent of youths recommended for transfer – more than four in five – had no prior record.[113]

This fact is alarming given researchers' consistent finding that ***the strongest predictor of future offending is a pattern of repeat offending: the commission of a single criminal act, no matter how serious, is not a strong indicator of future criminality. Meanwhile, many youth being transferred for violent offenses are not dangerous criminals.*** Statutes defining armed robbery and aggravated assault – which account for the great majority of violent index crime arrests – can include taking lunch money at the school cafeteria or a simple threat of violence, without any physical violence inflicted or even attempted. Moreover, laws in many states fail to differentiate guilt based on the role played by offenders in committing a crime. Most youth crime – unlike adult crime – is committed in groups, and often some members of a group play little or no role in planning and perpetrating the crime. In these cases, it makes little sense to transfer youth to criminal court.

Transfers to criminal court disproportionately target minority youth. All across the nation, minority youth are transferred to criminal courts at rates far beyond their prevalence in the general population, and far beyond their prevalence among those arrested and referred to juvenile court. As a result, 60 percent of juveniles admitted to adult prisons nationwide are African American, another 17 percent are other ethnic minorities (15 percent Hispanic, one percent Asian, one percent Native American), and 23 percent are white.[114] In the nation's 75 largest counties, 67 percent of juveniles tried as adults in criminal court are African American.[115] The disproportionate transfer rates for minority youth are especially pervasive with drug crimes: 75 percent of juvenile defendants charged with drug offenses in adult court are African American, and 95 percent of juveniles sentenced to adult prison for drug offenses are minorities.[116]

Race of Juveniles Admitted to State Prisons and Racial Composition of Overall Juvenile Population

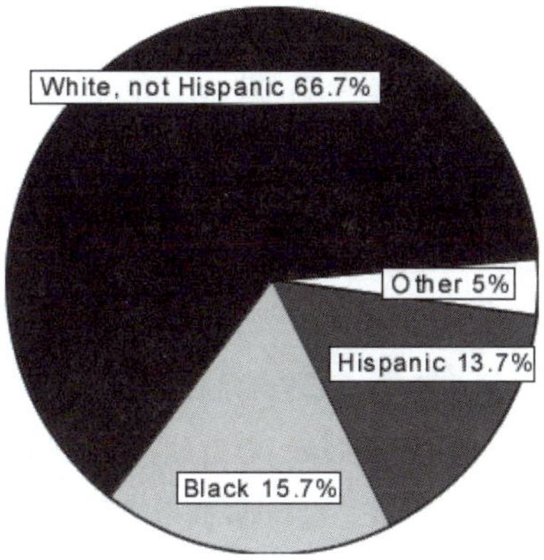

Source: U.S. Bureau of the Census, population estimates for 1998

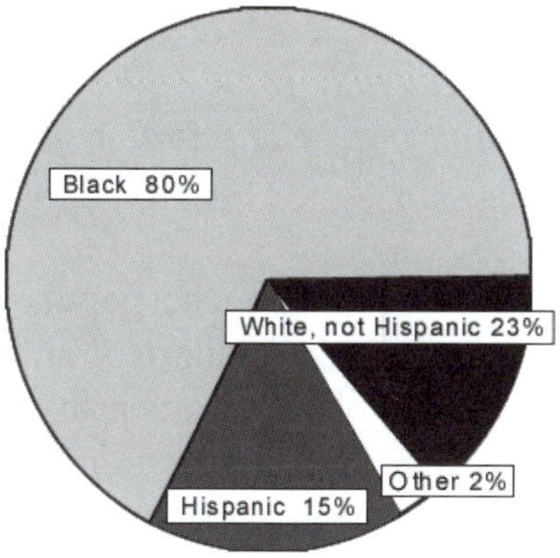

Source: *Juvenile Offenders and Victims: 1999 National Report* (Pittsburgh, PA: National Center for Juvenile Justice, 1999), p. 209

Transfer is expensive and wastes funds desperately needed to implement research-proven intervention programs. In addition to its impact on youth and minority communities, the widespread transfer of juvenile offenders also poses serious problems for the criminal justice system, and added costs for taxpayers as well. At the court level, criminal prosecutions require more hearings, involve more investigation and attorney preparation, result in more jury trials, and take at least twice as much time as comparable cases in juvenile court.[117] The majority of youths transferred to criminal court spend months awaiting trial in an adult jail cell or a juvenile detention center – with a cost to taxpayers of $100-$175 per day. The California Legislative Analyst's Office estimates that the new get-tough transfer provisions enacted by voters in March 2000 could cost taxpayers $100 million per year in added operating costs, plus $200-$300 million for construction of new jail cells.[118]

Aggressive transfer laws are not needed to stiffen punishments for the most egregious young offenders. Perhaps the most ironic fact about America's rush toward "adult time for adult crime" is that the stated goal – sharpening punishments for the most serious juvenile offenders – can be achieved without incurring the costs or imposing the collateral damage that come with transfers to criminal court. Historically, juvenile courts' jurisdiction over youthful offenders has ended at age 21 or younger in most states. Even for a cruel, pre-meditated murder, a young offender processed in juvenile court would be set free at an early age – even if the offender had a juvenile record a mile long. Over the past 15 years, however, several states have enacted "blended jurisdiction" statutes that allow juvenile courts to impose longer sentences on particularly serious offenders. Under these statutes, states typically offer youth a "last chance" before transferring them to the adult correctional system – suspending the adult sentences for youth who follow the rules, participate in treatment, and demonstrate the attitudes and skills necessary to stay crime-free. Thus, the state can impose serious sanctions on those who demonstrate little hope of rehabilitation, while allowing others to reform their delinquent behavior patterns without the lifelong stain of a criminal record.

A Question of Punishment.

From a practical point of view, the widespread transfer of youthful offenders to criminal courts fails virtually every test. It does not reduce recidivism. It does not deter crime. It creates immense collateral damage for individual youths, for communities, for taxpayers, and for the criminal justice system itself.

Why then does it remain such a popular option? Why do political leaders, reporters, and citizens ignore the evidence of transfer's negative impacts – or fail to ask hard-headed questions in the first place – and instead continue to support transfer for ever-larger numbers of youth?

Perhaps the key to this question was revealed in 1998 by Alabama Senator Jeff Sessions in an appearance on the ABC News "This Week" telecast following the school shooting tragedy in Jonesboro, Arkansas. Senator Sessions was "morally offended," he explained, that the youths involved in that episode could not be harshly punished because they remained under juvenile court jurisdiction. This desire to punish youthful offenders severely when they commit heinous crimes, this sense of moral outrage Senator Sessions shares with a substantial majority of American voters, goes to the heart of perhaps the most controversial aspect of the juvenile court during this century – limitations on punishment.

Throughout the history of the juvenile court, high profile cases have emerged in which youth accused of heinous crimes have been shielded from long punishments. In recent years, such high profile cases have combined in the public mind (and many political leaders' rhetoric) with a growing perception that juvenile courts are too lenient with youthful offenders. Given the mounting fears of teen crime, the desire to seek "just deserts" for teen criminals is understandable.

Ultimately, however, the "moral" arguments raised by those who advocate for more transfers to criminal court – while understandable – are unpersuasive. Through judicial waiver laws, juvenile courts already have the right to transfer the most egregious juvenile offenders. Those whom the courts do not have authority to transfer – the very young offenders – typically have not developed far enough intellectually to participate competently in their own defense, as our legal tradition requires. Moreover, "blended sentencing" options are available to the states to add teeth to the sanctions available in the juvenile courts without incurring the collateral damage associated with transfer to criminal jurisdiction.

. . . "blended sentencing" options are available to the states to add teeth to the sanctions available in the juvenile courts without incurring the collateral damage associated with transfer to criminal jurisdiction.

On the other hand, the case for retaining youth within the juvenile courts' jurisdiction is also bolstered by important moral principles, in addition to the many profound practical considerations detailed above.

Diminished capacity. Young people often lack the qualities that are typical in adults and critical to refraining from criminal conduct. "To the extent that new situations and opportunities require new habits of self-control, the teen years are periods when self-control issues are confronted on a series of distinctive new battlefields," writes criminologist Franklin Zimring. "New domains – including secondary education, sex, and driving – require not only cognitive appreciation of the need for self-control but also its practice. If this normally takes a while to develop, the bad decisions made along the way should not be punished as severely as the bad decisions of adults who have passed through the period [of] opportunity to develop habits of self-control."[119]

This lack of self-control is exacerbated by adolescents' acute sensitivity to peer pressure. Of all youth arrested for violent crimes in New York City in 1978, the great majority committed their crimes in groups. Sixty percent of juvenile assault arrestees, 78 percent of juvenile homicide arrestees, 86-90 percent of juvenile arrestees for robbery or burglary were accused of committing these crimes in tandem with at least one other offender.[120] By contrast, most adults commit such crimes alone. "Most adolescent decisions to break the law or not take place on a social stage where the immediate pressure of peers urging the adolescent is often the real motive for most teenage crime," Zimring noted. "A necessary condition for an adolescent to stay law-abiding is the ability to deflect or resist peer pressure. Many kids lack this crucial skill for a long time."[121]

Room to Reform. Given that a large slice of the adolescent population engages in wrongful conduct, and given that most youth will desist from crime as a natural consequence of their maturation into adulthood, ***the critical goal should be to punish these youth in ways that do not seriously damage their future life chances. Yes, youthful offenders should be punished and held accountable for their crimes. Yes, they deserve punishment, and indeed some form of punishment may be necessary to help youth mature and fully appreciate that their actions have consequences. In any enlightened approach to juvenile crime, the end result of this punishment should not be to isolate and ostracize young people but to teach them responsibility, advance their preparation for adulthood, and seek to reintegrate them successfully into the law-abiding community.***

Transferring youth to criminal court achieves just the opposite result. By staining young people with criminal records, by placing them side-by-side with adult criminals in state prisons where rehabilitation and youth development are not central goals, transfer only reduces the chances that delinquent youth will ever make the successful transition to adulthood. As a result, these youth will be at heightened risk to offend again, and the rest of us will be that much less safe.

The evidence is clear, the conclusions unavoidable. Wholesale transfer of delinquent youth to criminal courts is misguided policy.

Part Three: RE-INVENTING JUVENILE JUSTICE AND DELINQUENCY PREVENTION

The vast majority of youth who commit crimes are not serious, chronic, violent offenders, let alone "superpredators." Jettisoning these young people to criminal courts does more harm than good. Meanwhile, our nation's capacity to successfully prevent and treat delinquency grows each year. Together, these three realities point powerfully to the need in America for strong and scientific systems to address youth violence and delinquency.

Juvenile courts and corrections systems stand at ground zero in our nation's battle to rein in juvenile crime and stem the tide of adult criminals entering our society. They impact the lives of nearly three million young people arrested each year. With rapidly growing budgets measured in the billions, they consume an ever-increasing share of scarce taxpayer dollars for youth development and other social policy priorities. Yet, apart from the public uproar over adult time for adult crime, apart from an occasional expose about abuse or substandard conditions at one or another juvenile corrections institution, the media and the public pay little attention to juvenile justice. How efficient are the courts in treating and punishing juvenile offenders? How effective are juvenile probation and corrections agencies in helping turn around troubled youths and set them back on course? We ignore these questions at our peril.

Meanwhile, a number of prevention strategies have demonstrated power to substantially lower the number of young people who become delinquent. How widely are these strategies being utilized? How effective are the efforts currently underway to nip criminal careers in the bud? If we are to win the battle against juvenile crime, asking and answering these questions is a crucial first step.

Chapter Four
WORTHY OF THE NAME?
(How Well are America's Juvenile Justice Systems Doing the Job?)

On July 3, 1899, 11 year-old Henry Campbell's mother hauled him into a Chicago courtroom. He was charged only with petty larceny – and sentenced to go live at his grandmother's house – but Campbell's case rang in a judicial revolution. It was the first ever-adjudicated in a court of law dedicated exclusively to children.[122]

Until that time, children's fate in the justice system had been deplorable. Children were routinely jailed with adults, sentenced to labor, and often brutalized. In Chicago, the local jail held hundreds of children at the turn of the century, some as young as eight. Many came from the city's desperate tenement houses, arrested for stealing food or coal. The courts fined the children, though most had no money to pay, and then placed them in jail to work off their debts.[123]

Prodded by children's rights activists, Cook County established a juvenile court to end these abuses. The court created an entirely new system of justice based on the principle that children are inherently different than adults, less culpable for their acts and more amenable to rehabilitation. Under the unique rules of this new court, children would not be tried like adults through a formal, open and adversarial process. The goal would not be to punish wrongdoers for their crimes. Rather, the new court would operate as "a kind and just parent" to children, using closed and informal hearings to act in the best interests of the child.

The Juvenile Court was hailed as a breakthrough throughout the world. By 1915, 46 states, three territories and the District of Columbia had established Juvenile Courts.[124] By 1925, separate courts for children had been created in Great Britain, Canada, Switzerland, France, Belgium, Hungary, Croatia, Argentina, Austria, India, Holland, Madagascar, Japan, Germany, Brazil, and Spain.[125]

In many ways, these courts represented a big step forward for children. They shielded child prisoners from adult offenders, and they protected the privacy of young offenders, allowing them to enter adult life unhampered by criminal records. The courts hired probation counselors, psychologists and other staff to supervise and support young offenders, and in many courtrooms well-meaning judges and staff devised creative and uplifting programs for troubled children – both delinquent offenders and children victimized by abuse, neglect or abandonment.

Today, however, juvenile justice finds itself under fire in America, facing critics from both the left and the right of our political spectrum. Those on the right decry its "soft" response to crime and accuse juvenile courts of "coddling" instead of punishing dangerous young criminals. Those from the left decry the continued lack of legal safeguards for juvenile offenders, the unequal treatment of minorities, and the inhumane conditions of confinement in more than a handful of juvenile correctional institutions. Serious proposals to do away with the juvenile court have been issued by individuals on both sides of this ideological divide.

Given the dire consequences of prosecuting youth in criminal courts, given the great opportunities created by advances in prevention and intervention research, and given our nation's urgent need for youth-oriented crime prevention, these abolitionists clearly go too far. Our nation needs a juvenile justice system. The questions remain, however: How effective are today's juvenile courts and corrections systems? How well do they live up to the initial ideals of the juvenile justice movement. Do they provide justice worthy of the name?

Fifty-One Systems.

Because juvenile justice is primarily a state and local responsibility, there exists no single "juvenile justice system" in America. Rather, there are 51 state systems most of which are divided into local systems delivered through county courts and local probation offices and state correctional agencies and private service providers – each with its own rules and idiosyncracies. Thus, generalizing about juvenile justice in America is problematic. These systems do, however, have a common root and a common set of core principles that distinguish them from criminal courts for adult offenders.

- **Limited jurisdiction.** In most states, juvenile courts can prosecute offenders up to age 17. In 10 states the upper age is 16, and in three states the upper age is 15. All offenders above these ages are automatically tried as adults in criminal courts.

- **Informal proceedings**. In most states, verdicts are determined by judges, not juries. Legal representation for youthful offenders was a rarity until the 1960s. Still today, many youth waive their rights to counsel.

- **Focus on the offender, not the crime**. Youth prosecuted and found to have committed crimes are adjudicated "delinquent" rather than convicted of crimes. For those found delinquent, the state assumes the role of "*parens patriae*," or surrogate parent, assigning the child to a correctional or treatment regimen based upon a judge's decision regarding the best interests of the child.

- **Indeterminate sentences**. Historically and still in most states today, youth placed in corrections do not receive a term-limited sentence, but instead remain incarcerated for as long or short as a judge or the state parole board see fit, up until the youth reaches an upper age limit (typically 18 or 21).

- **Confidentiality**. In order to spare youth the life-long handicap of a criminal record for their mistakes made in childhood, juvenile courtrooms were not opened to the public during most of this century, the names of juvenile offenders were not revealed, and the records of juvenile offenders were typically sealed and later destroyed. In recent years, these protections have been scaled back in most states as the emphasis of public policy has shifted from protecting children to protecting the society from children.

Historically, juvenile courts have been closed to reporters and the public. First-hand examination of juvenile justice was prohibited. In the mid-1990s, however, two observers – Edward Humes and William Ayers – gained unusual access to juvenile courts. Both men took a year out of their lives and immersed themselves in the culture of juvenile justice – following the cases of young people, interviewing professionals and public officials. Sadly, Humes in Los Angeles and Ayers in Chicago both came away with a similar and sobering impression.

"In Los Angeles," Humes wrote in his 1996 book, *No Matter How Loud I Shout*, "the judges, prosecutors and defense attorneys can't remember individual kids anymore, or faces or histories. They look at you as if you're insane if you name a juvenile and ask what happened with

"In Los Angeles, the judges, prosecutors and defense attorneys can't remember individual kids anymore, or faces or histories. They look at you as if you're insane if you name a juvenile and ask what happened with his or her case . . . The kids have been reduced to categories."

his or her case... The kids have been reduced to categories. As a result, the fundamental question the Juvenile Court was designed to ask – What's the best way to deal with this individual kid – is often lost in the process... Kids walk free when they are in desperate need of being reined in. Others get hammered by harsh punishments, whether they deserve it or not."[126]

"Today, as the Juvenile Court approaches its centennial, it has become by all accounts an unfit parent," Ayers wrote in his 1997 volume, *A Kind and Just Parent*, "unable to see children as three-dimensional beings or to solve the problems they bring with them through the doors, incapable of addressing the complicated needs of families. The gap between the crises faced by families and youths in trouble and the capacity of the Juvenile Court to address them is vast and growing."[127]

Do these stark observations apply to juvenile courts everywhere in America? A hard-headed look at existing juvenile justice efforts around our nation reveals that deep problems exist and fundamental reforms are necessary. While good and excellent systems exist here and there throughout our nation, and some positive programs can be seen in the juvenile justice systems of most cities and towns, the prevailing currents in juvenile justice are troubling.

The most pressing problems in juvenile justice can be found in six key areas:

Overwhelmed Courts.

Juvenile justice was founded on the belief that children who get into trouble with the law deserve and require individualized treatment guided by caring, compassionate staff and expert judges. Yet, as Barry Krisberg and James F. Austin of the National Council on Crime and Delinquency explain, despite rhetoric "steeped in concepts such as 'compassionate care' and 'individualized treatment'... too often the reality is assembly-line justice in which large numbers of youngsters and their families are quickly 'disposed of' through a limited number of options that rarely are adequately funded."[128]

Particularly in the juvenile courts of major cities, most youth are shuttled through rapid-fire hearing processes in which they are scarcely known to the authorities in charge. ***In Chicago, the average amount of court time given to any case in Juvenile Court is twelve minutes, and each Juvenile Court judge makes a total of 110 decisions on a typical day.***[129] "This is what most Juvenile Court hearings look like," wrote Edward Humes in Los Angeles: "Little substance, much legal ritual, all flow control – the judge sits at his desk like an air-traffic controller."[130]

Though the average hearing takes only four or five minutes, Humes reported, these hearings typically occur after months of delay. Nearly half of all delinquency cases formally adjudicated in the juvenile courts of major cities nationwide take more than 90 days to process – the maximum standard suggested by professional organizations. These delays, which are often caused by bureaucratic inefficiencies as well as inadequate staffing, cripple the effectiveness of the court process for youth. That is because, in the words of the National District Attorney's Association, "Time is a major consideration in handling juvenile cases... The longer it takes, the more likely the juvenile wonders if anyone cares. The long-term message is lost on the child."[131]

Even more problematic than delays are the outcomes of many juvenile court cases. "The juvenile justice system is often so overwhelmed that juvenile offenders receive no meaningful interventions or consequences, even for relatively serious offenses," found the National Juvenile Justice Action Plan, published by the U.S. Justice Department in 1996. "This neglect serves neither rehabilitation nor accountability goals, and young people need to know that if they break the law, they will be held accountable. Clearly, a revitalized juvenile justice system that ensures immediate and appropriate accountability and sanctions is a key to reversing trends in juvenile violence."[132]

Glaring Imbalance Between Institutional and Community-Based Services.

The United States will spend at least $10 billion dollars this year on juvenile justice. The majority of these dollars pay for confinement of a small segment of the juvenile offender population. This leaves far too few resources for community-based programs, services and sanctions that engage, punish and treat young offenders in their homes and communities. The imbalance severely handicaps the ability of juvenile justice agencies to control juvenile crime.

Long-standing over-reliance on large correctional institutions. In most states, the biggest piece of the juvenile justice budget is spent on corrections, and the largest number of incarcerated youth are sent to "training schools," large correctional units typically housing 100 to 500 youth. Conditions of confinement are often poor, however, and the process of isolating youth exclusively with other delinquent peers tends to exacerbate rather than mitigate the law-breaking tendencies of youthful offenders.

The decision to sentence a young person to training school is typically justified based upon one of two rationales: (1) the youth is a danger to society and must be removed; or (2) it will teach the youth a needed lesson. Under the light of examination, however, neither of these rationales justifies the persistent choice of most states to allocate the lion's share of juvenile justice funding to training school incarceration.

Most youth placed into training schools are not dangerous criminals. Nationwide, only 27 percent of youthful offenders in out-of-home placements in October 1997 were guilty of violent felony crimes. The large majority of these placements were to correctional units, with the rest being residential treatment centers or group homes. (Three-fourths of all juveniles in custody are held in facilities with more than 30 residents, and 70 percent of youth in custody are held in locked facilities.[133]) A 1993 study of 28 states found that only 14 percent of offenders in correctional training schools were committed for violent felonies. More than half of the youthful offenders in state institutions were committed for property or drug crimes and were serving their first terms in a state

What Does America Spend for Juvenile Justice?

How much does America spend every year on juvenile justice and delinquency prevention? Good question. Unfortunately, one without a good answer. The federal Bureau of Justice Statistics maintains a complete annual data set on all criminal justice expenditures nationwide – law enforcement, courts, and corrections. Yet the data are only for adult courts and corrections. No data are compiled for juvenile justice expenditures. In 1988, the Bureau of Justice Statistics produced a one-time estimate, placing national spending to arrest, prosecute and detain juvenile offenders at $15 to $20 billion per year, including $2 billion per year to detain juvenile offenders. However, that analysis has not been repeated since 1988.

Likewise, many states do not maintain data even on total state spending for juvenile justice activities – never mind expenditures by local governments to support municipal and county courts, detention centers, and probation agencies. Thus, a reliable national estimate of national expenditures for juvenile justice does not now exist.

In October 1999, the National Association of State Budget Officers released the results of a national survey, *State Juvenile Justice Expenditures and Innovations*, updating a similar survey conducted in 1994. The survey calculated state, local and federal expenditures for residential placement, community programming, delinquency prevention and post-residential care, and identified a total of $4.22 billion in 1998 – up 65 percent from the $2.55 billion identified in 1994. This figure grossly understates actual spending, however. NASBO was unable to collect data from three states – Connecticut, Delaware, and Alaska – and omitted them entirely. Second, the estimates seriously undercounted state-level juvenile justice spending in several states. In Illinois, NASBO estimated total juvenile justice expenditures at $90,915 in 1998 – though state expenditures for juvenile corrections alone were $81 million dollars. The survey counted only $84 million for Maryland and $402 million for Florida in 1998, when official state budgets for juvenile justice in these states were $124 million and $512 million respectively.

Because NASBO surveyed only state-level agencies, its survey counted local juvenile justice spending only when it was part of a state match. As a result, NASBO identified only $351 million in local juvenile justice expenditures, even though localities are primarily responsible in most states for financing and operating juvenile courts, probation, pre-trial detention, and community-based programming for juvenile offenders. Just in California's 15 largest counties alone, local juvenile justice expenditures consumed $344 million in 1993-94. In Washington State, NASBO identified less than $600,000 in local juvenile justice expenditures, while the Washington State Institute for Public Policy calculated the cost of operating juvenile courts, probation operations and detention centers at $71.6 million in 1995.

So how much does America spend on juvenile justice? Unfortunately, the answer remains a mystery. However, from the data that are available it is clear that the figure for juvenile courts and corrections (not including primary prevention) exceeds $10 billion and may approach $15 billion per year. Despite the significant drop in juvenile crime since 1993, the figure continues to grow rapidly – threatening to eclipse budgets for other youth development activities such as after school programming, school-to-career programs, and youth employment.

institution.[134] Another study in the early 1990s used an objective public safety risk instrument to determine that 31 percent of the incarcerated youth in 14 states could safely be placed in less secure settings without risking community safety.[135]

Meanwhile, large training schools have never proved effective in rehabilitating youthful offenders or steering them from crime. Recidivism from large training schools is uniformly high. A follow-up study on youth released from Minnesota's two training schools in 1991 found that 91 percent were arrested within five years of release. In Maryland, a study of 947 youths released from correctional facilities in 1994 found that 82 percent were referred to juvenile or criminal courts within two and one-half years after release.[136] In Washington State, 59 percent of incarcerated youth re-offended within one year and 68 percent within two years.[137] In fact, ***virtually every study examining recidivism among youth sentenced to juvenile training schools in the past three decades has found that at least 50 to 70 percent of offenders are arrested within one or two years after release. Clearly, training schools are not derailing the criminal careers of youthful offenders.***

Even more troubling, some studies suggest that training school sentences actually ***increase*** recidivism in comparison to community-based sentences. In a 1978 study by researchers at Ohio State University, youthful offenders sent to training schools were rearrested far faster (average 4.8 months) than youthful offenders supervised in the community (average 12 months). Even after controlling for seriousness of offense and other variables the researchers concluded that "with all else controlled, there is a moderate to high *inverse* relationship between the severity of the sanction for the first [crime] and the time elapsed until the second arrest."[138] A 1995 South Carolina study found that 82 percent of males born in 1967 who served time in a juvenile corrections institution had adult criminal records by age 27, whereas only 40 percent of juvenile offenders who did not serve time in confinement had adult records at 27.[139] "It is exceedingly difficult to successfully punish, deter, and treat incarcerated juvenile offenders in large, locked, secure training schools that are operating over capacity; yet this is the norm in juvenile corrections nationwide," writes David Altschuler, a Johns Hopkins University criminologist.[140]

In the early 1970s, Massachusetts shut down all of its large training schools and placed 85 percent of youth committed to state corrections into small, non-locked community-based correctional units run by local nonprofit agencies. Recidivism rates remained low in relation to other states, and the youth in these unlocked

Most Serious Offenses of Youth Removed from Their Homes By Juvenile Courts, 1997

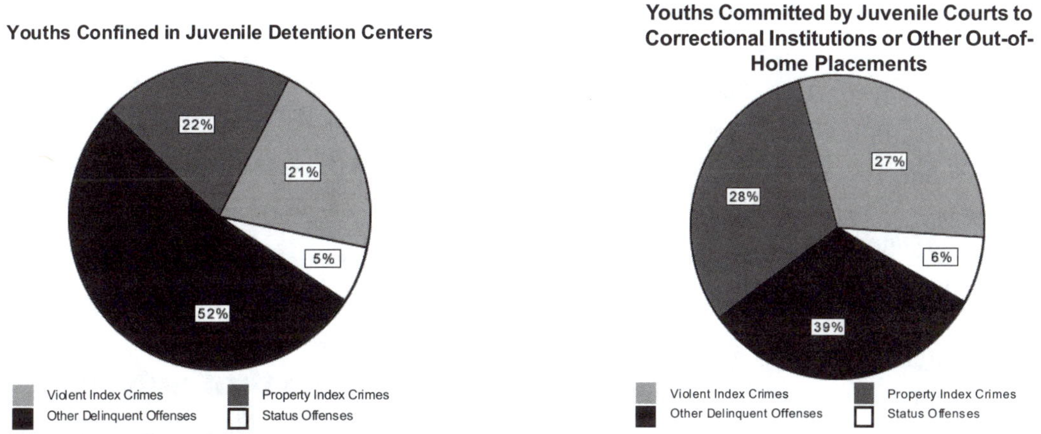

Violent Index Crimes include murder, rape, armed robbery and aggravated assault.
Property Index Crimes include burglary, theft, auto theft, and arson.

Source: Census of Juveniles in Residential Placement

A follow-up study on youth released from Minnesota's two training schools in 1991 found that 91 percent were arrested within five years of release. In Maryland, a study of 947 youths released from correctional facilities in 1994 found that 82 percent were referred to juvenile or criminal courts within two and one-half years after release.

facilities did not create serious crime problems in Massachusetts communities – committing just 1.3 percent of all crimes statewide. The new arrangement kept Massachusetts' overall juvenile crime rates among the lowest in the nation, while saving $11 million per year for state taxpayers.[141]

Following Massachusetts' example, Missouri closed the last of its training schools in 1983. In their place Missouri established 30 regional corrections centers, including unlocked residences, plus a variety of non-residential programs and services. These include "day treatment" centers (where young people receive intensive education, life skills training and/or family therapy) and intensive case monitoring projects pairing delinquent youth with college students who offer mentoring support and closely track delinquent youths' progress. Missouri's matrix of programs and services differs dramatically from the training school-oriented systems operating in most states. The results appear far better. Only 245 of 2,181 (11.2 percent) youth released from the state Division of Youth Services (DYS) from February 1998 through January 1999 were returned to DYS custody within one year of their release or transfer to a non-secure community corrections program (where they would have opportunity to offend).[142] Only eight percent of Missouri youth sentenced to juvenile corrections in 1991 were repeat commitments, and a follow-up study of nearly 5,000 Missouri youthful offenders released from DYS in the 1980s found that only 15 percent went on to collect adult criminal records.[143]

Despite this success, however, few states have followed Massachusetts' and Missouri's lead. "A century of experience with training schools and youth prisons demonstrates that they are the one extensively evaluated and clearly *ineffective* method to 'treat' delinquents," writes University of Minnesota law professor Barry Feld, one of the deans of juvenile justice theory and research. "Despite these consistent research findings, political leaders and correctional administrators rely on institutional controls and penal confinement with ever greater vengeance."[144]

Pervasive overutilization of juvenile detention. Analogous to jails in the criminal justice system, juvenile detention centers confine youth awaiting trials as well as those pending placement into a correctional program. Notwithstanding the wholesale drop in juvenile crime in recent years, the daily population of youth confined in juvenile detention centers has increased sharply – from 20,000 nationwide at the height of the juvenile crime wave in 1993 to some 24,500 youth in 1997. Seventy-nine percent of all youth held in detention in 1997 were not charged with violent index crimes. The decision whether or not to detain a young person is

Missouri's matrix of programs and services differs dramatically from the training school-oriented systems operating in most states. The results appear far better . . . a follow-up study of nearly 5,000 Missouri youthful offenders released . . . in the 1980s found that only 15 percent went on to collect adult criminal records.

not just a question of short-term liberty. It will also play a crucial role, experts say, in determining the ultimate disposition of the youth's case. "Children who are detained, rather than let go to their parents or released to some other program, are statistically much more likely to be incarcerated at the end of the process," says Mark Soler of the Youth Law Center in Washington, DC.[145] Detention decisions also have big implications for taxpayers, with a daily cost of $100-$175 per young person per day – for a total annual cost of almost $1 billion nationwide.[146] In many localities, operating the detention center consumes the lion's share of all dollars and person-hours devoted to juvenile justice.

Despite the impact on youth, however, and despite the heavy cost to taxpayers, the decision whether to hold a youthful offender in detention pending trial is often not based on strict and objective guidelines. Strong evidence suggests that in most jurisdictions many more young people are placed in detention than is necessary to protect public safety. For a fraction of the cost of detention, several alternative-to-detention strategies have shown great success keeping youth crime-free while they await trial and ensuring that youths appear at their court hearings. Some programs simply provide intensive supervision of youth released into the community. In Philadelphia, for instance, the Juvenile Justice Center, a local non-profit agency, contracts with the juvenile court to monitor 200 young people. The agency gets 85 percent of participants back to court without further arrests. Of the failures, two percent are arrested for a subsequent offense, three percent fail to appear for court date, and the remaining 10 percent are dropped from the program for going AWOL.[147] With a cost of just $12 to $30 per day – versus $310 per day in a Philadelphia detention center[148] – the program saves millions of dollars every year.

In addition to supervising youth awaiting trial, some alternatives-to-detention programs also help youth re-enroll in school if they've dropped out, provide needed counseling and services, and connect youth to tutoring or jobs or after-school programs. In Chicago, the Cook County Juvenile Probation Department has established six evening reporting centers since 1995 to provide after-school supervision of youth pending trial in juvenile court. Operated by community-based organizations from 4 p.m. until 8 p.m. every school day, these centers have offered a combination of supervision, recreation, academic tutoring and life skills instruction to more than 4,000 youth since 1995. Evening reporting centers cost only $33 per day per participant, compared with the $115 per day cost of Cook County's juvenile detention center, and 92 percent of all youth participating in the centers thus far have remained arrest-free until their appointed court date.[149]

For a fraction of the cost of detention, several alternative-to-detention strategies have shown great success keeping youth crime-free while they await trial and ensuring that youths appear at their court hearings.

Despite these successes, however, alternatives-to-detention programs are offered to only a small fraction of youthful offenders nationwide. In San Francisco, the Detention Diversion Advocacy Program described in Chapter One serves only 20 youth at a time, while the Juvenile Probation Department's "home detention" program serves only 122 youth per year. Meanwhile, San Francisco detained 3,285 of the 5,222 young people arrested citywide in 1998 (62.9 percent) – a rate far higher than other major cities in California or nationwide.[150]

Underinvestment in Community-Based Services.

In 1995, the U.S. Office of Juvenile Justice and Delinquency Prevention published a guide for its "Comprehensive Strategy for Serious, Chronic and

Violent Offenders," outlining the multiple components necessary for communities to effectively tackle the youth crime challenge.[151] These components included: 1) aggressive and research-driven prevention efforts; 2) a broad array of "graduated sanctions" in the community, including an immediate response to first offenses plus a range of intermediate sanctions and services for subsequent offending; and 3) corrections for those who pose a danger to society or fail repeatedly to respond positively to community-based sanctions.

Based on decades of best practice experience, this continuum approach has been endorsed by juvenile justice experts throughout the nation. However, conceptual agreement has not led to substantial redistribution of funding in most states and communities toward the first two elements of the continuum: prevention and graduated sanctions. As a result, juvenile justice systems throughout the nation continue to struggle – failing far more often than not in their efforts to address problem behaviors before they start or escalate.

Governor Christine Todd Whitman of New Jersey has described the core problem of juvenile justice this way: "A judge in one county has many options to craft appropriate orders for young offenders. In the next county over, especially if it is an urban county, a judge may have very few options between probation and incarceration. That's like choosing between aspirin or a lobotomy for a migraine."[152]

The vast majority of cases referred to the juvenile court do not result in incarceration. Instead, 43 percent are never petitioned, and two-fifths of those who are petitioned either have their cases dropped or subsequently sign an informal probation agreement. Finally, of the roughly one-third of cases that do result in a court finding of delinquency (i.e., a conviction) more than two-thirds result in probation, release, or alternative sanction. Thus, only 11 percent result in out-of-home placement to corrections or to a group home or residential treatment center. However, the majority of all juvenile justice funding in most states goes to confining and treating these 11 percent, while another large slice of the budget supports detention centers. In Maryland, for instance, only $36 million of the state's $136 million budget for juvenile justice in 1999 (27 percent) went to supervising or serving the 90 percent of youthful offenders not sentenced to an out-of-home placement.[153]

Juvenile courts theoretically have a wide range of options to appropriately punish youth not placed into corrections and to address any underlying problems that may be causing their delinquent behavior. These options can include restitution, community service, home curfew, academic tutoring, anger management training, individual or family counseling, substance abuse treatment, plus many others, or supervision by a probation officer without any of these activities. If a youth violates probation, the court might have a range of possible punishments – tightened curfew, added community service, more frequent drug testing, reduced privileges. Or the judge might have few of these options – as is too often the case. As Eric Joy, director of the Allegheny County (PA) juvenile courts, told a congressional committee in 1997, "Utilizing a system of progressive sanctions can be difficult if the means to carry them out are not available."[154]

"A judge in one county has many options to craft appropriate orders for young offenders. In the next county over, especially if it is an urban county, a judge may have very few options between probation and incarceration. That's like choosing between aspirin or a lobotomy for a migraine."

UNDERSTANDING THE JUVENILE COURT PROCESS

Arrest: When a minor is arrested, the police officer must decide whether to release the youth with a warning, sometimes called a "station adjustment," or refer the youth to juvenile court.

Intake: For youth referred to juvenile court, the first step is an "intake" process overseen by prosecutors in some jurisdictions and by staff of the juvenile probation department in other jurisdictions. At intake, a decision is made whether to file a "petition" in juvenile court (equivalent to filing charges in criminal court), drop the charges for lack of evidence, or handle the case informally.

Diversion: If the case is handled informally, staff in the probation department or the prosecutor's office will either release the young person without any further action, or propose a "diversion" plan in which the young person and his or her guardian agree to complete the terms of a behavioral contract as an alternative to formal adjudication in juvenile court. This contract might include informal supervision by probation staff as well as a curfew, restitution, community service, letter of apology, counseling, substance abuse treatment, or other requirements. If the youth completes the contract successfully, the charges are dropped; if the contract is not completed, the court may go ahead with a formal petition.

Detention: If the case is formally petitioned, the next decision made at intake is whether to hold the youth in confinement or release him or her to a parent or guardian pending trial. The legal reasons for holding a youth should be limited either to: a) safety (does the youth pose a threat to self or others?); or b) risk of flight (is the youth a risk to flee and not appear at scheduled hearings?). If the intake staff hold the young person in detention, a hearing is scheduled within 24 to 72 hours so that a judge can review the case and determine whether detention is warranted for the remaining time until the youth's adjudicatory hearing (see below). Bail is not generally available for youth detained by juvenile courts.

Transfer/Waiver: Youth accused of particularly serious crimes or with a record of chronic juvenile offending may be deemed unfit for juvenile court and instead "waived" or "transferred" to an adult criminal court. Transfers can be accomplished either through judicial waiver or through "direct file" by prosecutors (in some states). Youth accused of particularly serious crimes may be "excluded" from juvenile court and transferred automatically to adult criminal courts.

Adjudication: Trials in juvenile court are called "adjudicatory hearings," and the outcomes are typically decided by a judge rather than a jury. In these hearings, youth may admit or deny the petition of delinquency. When youth deny the petition, the judge may dismiss the case or adjudicate the youth as "delinquent" based on evidence presented by prosecutors and defense.

Disposition: Sentencing for those youth who are adjudicated delinquent is determined in a "disposition" hearing. After reviewing recommendations from probation staff (and sometimes from prosecutors and/or defense counsel), the judge issues a disposition order. This might include incarceration in a correctional training school (i.e., a youth prison), placement in a boot camp or wilderness challenge program, a therapeutic out-of-home placement, such as a group home or residential treatment center, a non-residential treatment or youth development program, general probation, or simple release. Traditionally, the period for which a delinquent youth remains in custody or on probation is indeterminate, and the length of stay is reviewed repeatedly based on the youth's progress in a treatment or rehabilitation program.

Aftercare: Traditionally a weak link in juvenile justice systems, "aftercare" is the juvenile justice term for post-release parole. Increasingly, aftercare is perceived as a critical element in juvenile justice programming, because many youth are unable to maintain the behavioral gains made in correctional and other residential programs when they return to the environments that fostered their delinquent conduct to begin with.

Corresponding Terminology in Juvenile Court and Criminal Court

Juvenile	Criminal
Petition	File Charges
Adjudicatory Hearing	Trial
Found Delinquent	Found Guilty
Disposition	Sentencing
Detention	Jail
Training School	Prison
Aftercare	Parole

Lack of juvenile probation staff is also a pervasive problem in many jurisdictions. "Currently, large numbers of probationers on county caseloads go essentially unsupervised because available resources are no match for the multitude of cases," wrote the California Youth Authority in 1994, reporting a truth that has changed little in most parts of California and that describes juvenile justice reality in many other parts of the country. "Minimum supervision/service and 'paper' caseloads predominate; and in general even 'supervised' probationers are rarely seen by a probation officer."[155]

Lack of Intensive Non-Residential Sanctions and Services. Following their court hearings, youth who are adjudicated "delinquent" (i.e., found guilty) have historically been: 1) sentenced to a correctional facility, 2) sent to a treatment center or group home, 3) placed on intensive probation supervision (usually home confinement with frequent checks by probation staff and sometimes electronic monitoring), 4) placed on regular probation (less frequent monitoring usually with orders for community service, restitution, counseling, curfew, and/or academic tutoring), or 5) released with a warning.

One disposition that historically has not been available in most communities, or has been used only for a select few, is intensive non-residential treatment and youth development services. This gap is not due to a lack of willingness on the part of juvenile courts and probation agencies to invest in treatment programs; rather, most jurisdictions regularly place troubled youth into group homes and residential treatment programs, often paying $200-or-more per day for these services.

This gap is especially striking given the tremendous success achieved by intensive non-residential programs, such as Multisystemic Therapy and Functional Family Therapy, two models highlighted at the top of this report. Both cost a small fraction as much as out-of-home placements to corrections or residential treatment, and both have achieved far greater success in resolving behavior problems and reducing recidivism. Despite successes

Case Outcomes for Youth Referred to Juvenile Courts in 1997

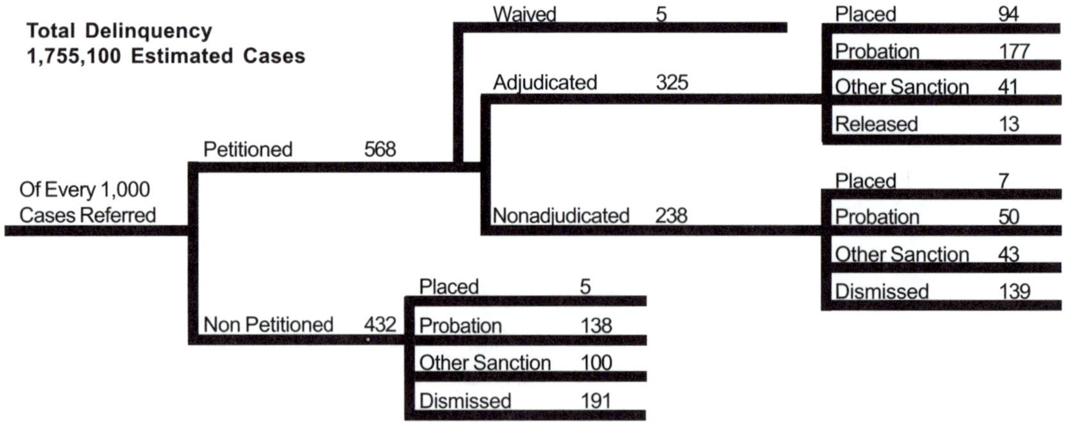

- *Waived* – Transferred to criminal court
- *Petitioned* – formally charged in juvenile court
- *Nonpetitioned* – case was dismissed or processed informally (with the juvenile and his/her family agreeing voluntarily to treatment or sanctions, without a formal hearing or finding of guilt)
- *Placed* – committed to a juvenile corrections facility or to a group home, residential treatment center, or foster home

Source: OJJDP Statistical Briefing Book. Online. Available: http://ojjdp.ncjrs.org/ojstatbb/delinquencytotal.html.

stretching over 14 years, and despite a price tag ($4,500 per youth) less than one-sixth the cost of an eight-month stint in juvenile corrections, MST will serve just 5,000 young people in 2000 – even though it has set up a corporation to assist with replicating the model anywhere in the nation.[156] Functional Family Therapy faces similar neglect. Despite nine successful clinical trials dating back to 1973, FFT programs will also serve just 5,000 young people in 2000 in a nation that arrests almost three million young people each year and locks up 105,000 on any given day.[157] Functional Family Therapy costs just $2,000 per youth, far less expensive than incarceration or placement in a group home.

Lack of Effective Aftercare. Of all the weaknesses in the arsenal of local juvenile justice systems nationwide, perhaps the most self-defeating is the lack of support and supervision for youth returning home from juvenile correctional institutions. By definition, these are the most dangerous and high-risk of all youth, yet in the vast majority of states and communities, these young people are provided only modest supervision as they re-enter the community and few services and supports to help them achieve success and remain crime-free.

In December 1999, the *Baltimore Sun* caused a political uproar in Maryland with a series of front-page stories about the state's juvenile justice system. While most of the reaction focused on reports of physical abuse of youth by staff at one correctional boot camp, the reporter also took time to document the anemic efforts made by the state to assist youth after completing their sentence. "That's how it works for many kids the state's juvenile justice system returns to the streets," the reporter found. "They're enrolled in after-care programs but immediately revert to running free, refusing to see their probation officers, blowing off drug and alcohol abuse classes, skipping town altogether, playing juvenile justice workers like they've set the rules."[158]

Throughout the country, aftercare efforts are crippled by a lack of coordination between staff at juvenile corrections institutions and those working in communities. In most states, aftercare is overseen by parole officers in the state corrections agency, not by local courts and probation staff rooted in the community. However, effective aftercare programming requires active collaboration among many partners – judges, aftercare agencies, schools, community-based organizations, probation agencies, and police. "The sheer size and organizational complexity of the juvenile 'justice system' make it exceedingly difficult to achieve basic communication, much less cooperation," explains David Altschuler. "The complexity and fragmentation of the system works against reintegration of offenders back into the community."[159]

Lack of Constructive Attention to Early Offenders. "The lack of consistent intervention with juvenile offenders soon after their initial contact with the police or other authorities has long been recognized as perhaps the single largest gap in services for troubled youth," writes the National Council on Crime and Delinquency (NCCD).[160] Unless they have committed serious crimes, most first offenders and even second offenders are released from the juvenile court without trial under a diversion or informal probation agreement. These dispositions may require community service or restitution, evening curfews, counseling or other programs. However, in many communities these agreements are not closely monitored. Courts "may

Of all the weaknesses in the arsenal of local juvenile justice systems nationwide, perhaps the most self-defeating is the lack of support and supervision for youth returning home from juvenile correctional institutions.

let offenders off without significant consequences," explains NCCD. "The system may also shunt youth into ordinary probation in overburdened agencies that are unable to provide supervision or support."[161]

Most first offenders never reappear in juvenile court. But for those who do re-offend, the lack of timely and consistent responses from probation staff and the court teaches the unfortunate lesson that the system is not serious – and the rules need not be heeded. The result, as NCCD reports, can be an " all-too-common pattern: several encounters with authorities; short-term detentions with no coherent, intensive interventions; repeated offenses; and eventual incarceration in juvenile and adult correctional facilities."[162]

Research has clearly identified the critical risk factors for chronic delinquency – early age at first arrest, early conduct problems, history of child abuse/neglect, low attachment and poor performance in school, chaotic families, substance abuse, and association with delinquent peers. Yet despite the success of Orange County, California's "8 Percent Solution" program, few jurisdictions operate intensive early intervention programs to work with youth at serious risk to become chronic offenders. In fact, most communities do not carefully investigate early offenders to determine if they are at serious risk.

Inattention to Research and Results.

Failure to replicate successful intervention models like Multisystemic Therapy, Functional Family Therapy, and the "8 Percent Solution" represents one of the great failures of our nation's juvenile justice system in recent years. Unfortunately, this failure is just one indication among many that a troubling lack of attention to results pervades juvenile justice programming in many parts of our nation.

"To date, most of the resources committed to the prevention and control of youth violence, both at the national and local levels, have been invested in untested programs based on questionable assumptions and delivered with little consistency or quality control," writes Dr. Delbert Elliott, director of the Center for the Study and Prevention of Violence in Boulder, Colorado. "This means we will never know which (if any) of them have had some significant deterrent effect; we will learn nothing from our investments in these programs to improve our understanding of the causes of violence or to guide our future efforts to deter violence; and there will be no real accountability for the expenditures of scarce community resources."[163]

Feeble Efforts to Collect Data and Monitor Results. As Elliott suggests, the lack of quality information about juvenile justice programs and systems can be striking. At the national level, we have no reliable data regarding the total level of funding for juvenile justice efforts. In other words, there exists no reliable estimate of what we are spending as a nation to tackle a problem that has topped the list of voter concerns for much of the past decade.

At the state level, only 26 states collect or publish any data on recidivism by youth returning to the community from training schools and other corrections programs,[164] and only a small fraction of cities nationwide monitor the subsequent offending of youth placed into various programs and dispositions. Most contracted service providers in juvenile justice are paid through cost-reimbursement contracts that offer no rewards for meeting outcome goals. In many cases, there are no outcome goals – only agreements regarding services to be provided. In 1998, the Florida Department of Juvenile Justice surveyed states to determine how they evaluate the success of programs they fund with $87 million provided each year from the federal Office of Juvenile Justice and Delinquency Prevention. Of the 46 states contacted, only eight require funded programs to report on a specific set of outcome measures, and only Florida produces an annual summary of results. Eighteen states monitor the programs less than once per year.[165]

A 1999 report from the Legislative Auditor's Office in Minnesota illustrates how unconcerned with results juvenile justice leaders can be: only seven percent of county-level juvenile justice agencies in Minnesota maintain any information on the subsequent success of youth ordered into out-of-home residential placements. (These include both delinquents and youth in the child welfare system). Despite the fact that these placements consume $225 million per year in the state and provide more than three million care-days per year, only 32 percent of juvenile corrections supervisors believe that residential service providers should be held more accountable than they are now.[166]

Extensive Funding of Demonstrably Ineffective Services. This lack of attention to results is particularly worrisome in light of the evidence that many programs and services to attack delinquency don't work. As Elliott explains, "Some of the most popular programs have actually been demonstrated in careful scientific studies to be *ineffective*, and yet we continue to invest huge sums of money in them for largely political reasons."[167]

Juvenile "boot camps" provide one example. Based on a popular notion that delinquent youths and criminal adults need a strong dose of character and discipline, correctional boot camps emerged throughout the nation during the 1980s and '90s. However, a series of scientific evaluations found that juvenile boot camps, as operated in most jurisdictions, simply don't work. In virtually every study, recidivism has been as high or higher for boot camp graduates as for participants in traditional corrections and probation programs. "Data from around the U.S. show that bootcamps have not produced a decrease in the number of bootcamp graduates who are rearrested for other crimes," reported the Kansas-based Koch Crime Comission in 1998, and recidivism rates range from 64 to 75 percent nationwide.[168] Yet, while a handfull of boot camps have been shut down in recent years, most continue to operate as usual.

"To date, most of the resources committed to the prevention and control of youth violence, both at the national and local levels, have been invested in untested programs based on questionable assumptions and delivered with little consistency or quality control."

Despite powerful evidence that parenting practices and the home environment play a vital role in controlling or fostering delinquent behavior by adolescents, juvenile justice agencies offer in-depth family therapy for relatively few youth, and the therapy they do provide often lacks focus and intensity. Meanwhile, traditional insight-oriented individual and group psychotherapy remain a staple of juvenile justice treatments, despite consistent findings that these conventional modes of therapy produce no effect on subsequent offending.

Perhaps the most powerful reason for increasing the focus on results in juvenile justice programming is that sometimes, despite good intentions, programs for delinquent teens actually exacerbate offending. When Mark Lipsey of Vanderbilt University reviewed findings of 443 controlled evaluations of juvenile justice intervention projects, he found that 30 percent showed an overall counterproductive effect.[169] Transfers to criminal court offer one example – raising rather than lowering the recidivism rates of youthful offenders. Programs that assemble high-risk youth for group activities also frequently exacerbate delinquency, a dynamic many researchers attribute to the development of stronger ties among delinquent youth involved in the programs. As University of Maryland criminologist Denise Gottfredson has written, "Interventions that group high-risk youths with lower-risk youths in the absence of a strong intervention to establish pro-social group norms often backfire."[170] Both in and out of correctional institutions, however, these group approaches remain one of the most common modes of juvenile justice programming.

Counterproductive "Net-Widening."

Early in the 1999-2000 school year, a group of Mississippi high school students were throwing peanuts at one another on a school bus. One of the peanuts hit the bus driver. The driver immediately pulled over the bus, and phoned the police. When police officers arrived at the scene, they diverted the bus to the courthouse, and then arrested five students for felony assault, which carries a five-year maximum sentence. The young men were also suspended from school, and their bus privileges were withdrawn. Eventually, after the students engaged an attorney, the criminal charges were dropped. However, all five students had to drop out of school due to lack of transportation.[171]

A 13-year-old boy in Denton County, Texas was assigned to write a "scary" Halloween story as a class assignment. He wrote a tale about shooting up a school, turned in the story, and received a passing grade. He was then called into the principal's office, police were called, and the boy found himself in jail for six days before the courts confirmed that no crime had been committed.[172]

A 10-year-old in Arlington, Virginia put soapy water into his teacher's drink. The school not only suspended the boy for three days, but also called the police, who charged him with a felony carrying a maximum sentence of 20 years. The boy was formally charged in juvenile court, though the case was ultimately dropped several months later.[173]

These stories are part of a disturbing trend in juvenile justice – an increasing tendency to arrest young people and to prosecute them for behavior that has traditionally been addressed informally. Despite the substantial decline in serious crimes committed by young people that began in 1993, the total youth arrest rate climbed from 8,438 arrests per 100,000 youth ages 10-17 in 1993 to 9,219 per 100,000 youth in 1997. While arrests for violent index crimes dropped 20 percent and index property crimes declined six percent from 1993 to 1997, they grew by 17 percent for simple assault, 30 percent for disorderly conduct, 73 percent for drug abuse violations (mostly for possession), and 77 percent for curfew violations. The trend finally began to reverse in 1998, with arrest rates declining in most offense categories.[174]

Referrals to juvenile courts also rose during this period of decreasing crime, climbing from an estimated 1.48 million cases in 1993 to 1.76 million in 1997. The greatest increases came in less serious offenses such as disorderly conduct (up 38 percent), simple assault (up 45 percent), obstruction of justice (51 percent), and drug law violations (105 percent). Yet the number of cases formally adjudicated in juvenile courts increased far more quickly (up 26 percent) than the number of cases handled informally (only 10 percent). Despite the less serious offending, the number of youth placed into secure detention increased from 1993 to 1997.[175]

Is there any benefit to public safety from prosecuting a 12-year-old girl for breaking a friend's violin – as recently occurred in Denver, Colorado? The evidence suggests that there is not. By swelling the caseloads of juvenile courts and probation agencies, aggressive prosecution of minor offending reduces the already-inadequate capacity of juvenile courts to effectively supervise and serve youth with higher risks to re-offend. Further, suggests David Altschuler, "lower-risk offenders subjected to high levels of supervision tend to do worse than if supervised less intensively."[176] When David Farrington, a British criminologist, compared a group of teenagers convicted of delinquency with a demographically matched group who had engaged in similar acts but had not been adjudicated delinquent, he found that those convicted were

By swelling the caseloads of juvenile courts and probation agencies, aggressive prosecution of minor offending reduces the already-inadequate capacity of juvenile courts to effectively supervise and serve youth with higher risks to re-offend.

"significantly more likely to engage in delinquency at a later age."[177]

Violations of Adolescents' Civil and Human Rights.

When it was first conceived at the turn of the last century, the juvenile court was hailed throughout the world as a major step forward in the treatment of youth. Indeed, prior to the juvenile court the treatment of young people in the criminal justice system was abysmal: youngsters were often prosecuted and sent to the prison or the "poor house" alongside adult prisoners, confined in subhuman conditions and commonly abused. Sadly, these violations of children's rights did not end with the coming of the juvenile court. Today, many serious rights issues remain.

Disproportionate minority confinement. The facts are unavoidable: at every stage of the juvenile justice process, minority youth – and African Americans in particular – are treated more harshly than white youth.

African American youth constitute only 15 percent of the U.S. population ages 10 to 17, but they account for:[178]

- **26 percent of juvenile arrests nationwide;**
- **30 percent of delinquency referrals to juvenile courts;**
- **33 percent of delinquency cases formally petitioned (i.e., charged) in juvenile court;**
- **40 percent of juveniles committed to out-of-home placements by juvenile courts;**
- **45 percent of all youth held in juvenile detention;**
- **46 percent of juveniles waived to criminal court; and**
- **60 percent of juveniles serving time in adult prisons.**

In Wisconsin, minorities are 19 percent of juveniles arrested and 75 percent of juveniles locked up in adult prisons. In Pennsylvania, minorities constitute 30 percent of juvenile arrests but 87 percent of juveniles in secure corrections. In both Connecticut and Texas, 100 percent of the juveniles held in adult jails in 1996 were minorities.[179] According to a 1991 review, two-thirds of studies examining minority treatment in juvenile justice find that even controlling for differences in seriousness of offense or prior offending history, the juvenile justice system treats non-white children more harshly.[180]

In 1992, the U.S. Congress took a significant step to address the disproportionate minority confinement challenge – requiring states to examine their policies for racial bias and take steps to eliminate it. In its first seven years, this measure helped produce encouraging results: African Americans declined from 52 percent of transferred cases nationally to 46 percent, and from 43 percent of delinquency cases resulting in residential placements to 36 percent.[181] Despite this success, however, the U.S. Senate voted in 1999 to eliminate the provision from the federal juvenile justice law. In May 2000, that Senate bill remained in conference committee, where it must be reconciled with a House of Representatives bill that retains the provision.

Lack of effective representation and due process protections. Until the 1960s, youthful offenders had no constitutional right to counsel, and legal representation was rare. The Supreme

The facts are unavoidable: at every stage of the juvenile justice process, minority youth – and African Americans in particular – are treated more harshly than white youth.

Court granted youths the right to counsel in 1967; however, its ruling allowed youth to waive this right, and the Court offered no guidelines for courts to ensure that young people are fully informed before waiving counsel. As a result, in some jurisdictions fewer than half of all youth adjudicated in juvenile court are represented by counsel.[182] This lack of counsel is especially concerning today, when many states are making prior juvenile adjudications a factor in future sentencing decisions. Similarly, while young people are advised of their rights to remain silent, they are also permitted in most states to waive that right without benefit of counsel – and many do, freely admitting to crimes without clearly understanding the ramifications of their confessions.

Substandard conditions of confinement. In 1993 the U.S. Justice Department released a comprehensive study on conditions in the juvenile detention and correctional centers across the country. Its findings: the vast majority of youth are held in facilities that do not meet basic standards, with endemic overcrowding the most prevalent problem. Sixty-two percent of incarcerated youth were held in overcrowded facilities, which suffer higher rates of violence against both staff and other youth than non-crowded facilities.[183] Lawsuits in many states and cities have challenged the lack of educational programming for youth, lack of access to services for those with learning disabilities or other special needs, and excessive violence in the imposition of discipline by correctional staff. Most troubling are cases of physical abuse by juvenile corrections staff.

"Troubled youths in state custody face 'lesson-teaching' beatings, filthy quarters, cramped cells, unwanted sex and caretakers who don't care," read the June 1998 headline of an *Arkansas Democrat-Gazette* expose on conditions in that state's juvenile correction system.[184] In Louisiana's Tellulah youth facility, the subject of a *New York Times* feature in 1998, "inmates of the privately-run prison regularly appear at the infirmary with black eyes, broken noses or jaws or perforated eardrums from beatings by the poorly paid, poorly trained guards or from fights with other boys."[185] Overall, 37 successful lawsuits have been filed on behalf of juvenile offenders in 25 states in the past three decades regarding both overcrowding and abuse issues, and the problems show no sign of abating.[186]

A Bird's Eye View: Juvenile Justice in Seven Urban Areas.

From the literature on juvenile justice, it is clear that our nation's juvenile justice apparatus faces many challenges. But how pervasive are these problems? How much do the problems affect the treatment of young people and how severely do they limit the effectiveness of local systems?

To answer these questions, the author traveled to several cities nationwide to interview experts and officials and gather available data. In each city he found leaders who are committed to the rehabilitative mission of juvenile justice, and in each jurisdiction at least the aura of change could be detected. At the same time, however, these visits confirmed that most of the issues and challenges detailed above plague juvenile justice efforts in every locality.

- One of the first communities in the nation to receive federal funding to implement the "comprehensive strategy" against juvenile violence, **San Diego County** has mounted a comprehensive campaign to enhance local programming to prevent and respond to delinquency. It created intensive full-day programs for high-risk first offenders and for youth at risk of out-of-home placements, significantly expanded adolescent substance abuse treatment, boosted after-school programming, and developed comprehensive community centers to serve youth and their families. While far more extensive than the services offered in most jurisdictions, however, these model programs still serve only a fraction of the juvenile population that could benefit. San Diego's detention population continues to exceed capacity, largely because the city has not developed a set of strong alternatives to detention programs.

- The City and County of **San Francisco** are developing an intensive program evaluation system to closely track results for each of its programs serving delinquent youth. And San Francisco is beginning to replicate the "8 percent" early intervention strategy pioneered in Orange County, California. Yet ambitious plans for a public-private partnership to fundamentally overhaul the San Francisco's juvenile justice intake process have made little headway since they were announced in 1997, and San Francisco continues to detain an alarmingly high percentage of youth referred to juvenile court – diverting few youth to alternatives-to-detention programs.

- Despite opening a new detention facility in 1991, **King County (Seattle), Washington** was again plagued in the late 1990s with overcrowding that threatened to require construction of a second detention center by 2005 at a cost of more than $11 million. The crowding was due partly to the fact that the State of Washington has begun to allow detention of truants, runaways, and other status offenders – in violation of the core mandate of the federal juvenile justice act. The overcrowding problem prompted an intensive review by consultants and staff at the county juvenile justice agency, and this study effort has yielded a series of reform initiatives that include implementation of Multisystemic Therapy and Functional Family Therapy as well as renewed efforts to limit detention for status offenders. Thanks to these reform efforts, King County's detention population declined in 1999 for the first time in years, and plans for the second detention center have been shelved.

- **Tarrant County (Fort Worth), Texas** has built perhaps the most impressive array of community-based alternatives-to-detention and out-of-home placement in the nation, including treatment foster care, wraparound services, and extensive alternatives-to-detention programs. These programs have enabled the county to sharply limit the number of confined youth while providing intensive services and supervision to many youth in the community. Yet Tarrant County does not track the recidivism rates of participants beyond the initial probation period, and thus has no way to know the long-term success of its efforts in controlling crime.

- **Dallas County, Texas** takes an entirely different approach. Though its population is only 50 percent larger than neighboring Tarrant County, Dallas held four times as many youth in detention each day in 1998 (223 vs. 56). Dallas County also operates two local correctional facilities with capacity for 184 youth (Tarrant operates no such facilities), and still commits many more youthful offenders to the Texas Youth Authority each year. Dallas does, however, have a very strong data collection system and closely tracks the status of youth in every probation program. Dallas County's local budget for juvenile justice is $42 million per year – almost three times the $15 million budget for Tarrant County.

- After participating in a national detention reform initiative in the 1990s, **Cook County (Chicago), Illinois** has reduced the population in its once overcrowded juvenile hall – using new community-based "evening reporting centers" and other alternative programs to supervise youth who would otherwise be detained. The city's district attorney spearheaded the enactment of a new state juvenile justice law in 1998 that focuses on "restorative justice," and the city is now building community teams citywide to adjudicate young offenders in their own neighborhoods. By many accounts, however, Cook County's juvenile justice system remains overwhelmed by the volume of its caseload. As William Ayers concluded in his 1997 book about juvenile justice in Chicago, "The court is pervaded by a feeling of futility and despair. Starved for funds, lacking community programs, appropriate opportunities for children, and the minimal resources to discharge its responsibilities, Juvenile Court has become entangled in self-interested bureaucracies, balkanized by the clash of competing fiefdoms."[187]

- Operated by a statewide juvenile justice agency that was rocked by scandal in December 1999 over reports of physical abuse of youth by correctional staff, the juvenile justice system in **Baltimore, Maryland** is deeply troubled – a desperately overcrowded, 128-year-old detention center located 45 minutes from the city, few strong alternative-to-detention programs, inadequate funding for community-based programs, and an anemic aftercare system for those returning from correctional placements. A blue-ribbon task force reported in February 2000 that: 1) Maryland's juvenile justice agency "has serious management and operational deficiencies that have persisted for years;" 2) "probation services (for non-committed youth) are ineffectively planned and implemented, inadequately funded, and failed to significantly influence the delinquency careers of youth;" and 3) "almost two-thirds of currently committed youth would stay in the community if an objective classification system were used."[188] However, a handful of promising efforts are underway – a specialized program for female offenders (whose numbers are rising dramatically in Baltimore and nationwide), a young offenders project for 8-12 year-olds, and public defender advocacy project in which defenders identify alternatives for youth unnecessarily placed in detention.

Winds of positive change are blowing in juvenile justice. In most cases, however, reform efforts remain isolated or run up against solid walls of resistance. The problem is not primarily a lack of resources. Rather, in many communities stronger leadership is needed – a single-minded focus on reducing juvenile crime, lowering recidivism, improving cost-effectiveness, and fostering success among youth.

Chapter Five

THE AMBULANCE OR THE FENCE?

(Common Practice Versus Best Practice in Delinquency Prevention)

A stronger, smarter, more balanced juvenile justice system can make a crucial difference in controlling youth crime and halting the progression of adult criminal careers. Even the best juvenile justice system, however, can be only a second line of defense against youth crime. The most successful juvenile justice strategies, under ideal laboratory conditions, reduce future offending rates by only about 50 percent – and then only through effective delivery of complex, multi-dimensional, sustained and resource-intensive intervention methods. Far better is to *prevent* delinquency behaviors from occurring in the first place. In the words of University of Washington criminologists J. David Hawkins and Richard Catalano, attempting to reduce crime by focusing only on law enforcement and corrections is like "providing expensive ambulances at the bottom of a cliff to pick up the youngsters who fall off, rather than building a fence at the top of the cliff to keep them from falling in the first place."[189]

. . . attempting to reduce crime by focusing only on law enforcement and corrections is like "providing expensive ambulances at the bottom of a cliff to pick up the youngsters who fall off, rather than building a fence at the top of the cliff to keep them from falling in the first place."

As detailed in Chapter One, social scientists have developed an impressive repertoire of intervention techniques over the past two decades to prevent the onset of delinquency. However, taking advantage of these advances requires that funds be appropriated, and that well-designed approaches be selected and implemented thoroughly and with care. While public spending has increased in recent years for prevention activities, thanks to growing public concerns over youth violence, too few resources are being applied to programs that research shows actually work.

Prevention in Early Childhood.

Despite the dramatic impact demonstrated by early intervention programs for children in high-risk families, no state and no city in America has implemented intensive home visitation services for all high-risk families. The State of Hawaii has come the closest, funding a state Healthy Start home visitation initiative that serves roughly 40 percent of infants born to high-risk families statewide.[190] Many cities and states have also implemented pilot home visitation projects in recent years. Yet none comprehensively serves all or most high-risk mothers.

Also, some jurisdictions have attempted to meet the early childhood needs of high-risk families by offering indirect support through case management to help families identify needs and access existing service providers in their communities – rather than providing needed parenting support, health services, and educational child care directly. From 1989 to 1994 the U.S. Department Health and Human Services funded an ambitious demonstration project designed to test the impact of intensive case management support and service referrals on the success of low-income children and their families. A carefully controlled evaluation found that the project "did not produce any important positive effects on participating families."[191] The 2,200 families who received these services in

21 demonstration sites had no better outcomes in economic self-sufficiency for families or cognitive or emotional development for children than an equal number of non-participating families – despite a price-tag of $45,000 per family. Evaluators found that the initiative was implemented as designed, and proved "that the case management approach does not lead to improved outcomes for parents and children."[192]

Despite a long track record, the federal Head Start program still serves only half of all eligible low-income pre-school children nationwide. Moreover, Head Start as currently operated typically lacks critical features such as highly educated staff and intensive home visitation and family involvement that produced the powerful impacts documented by the Perry Preschool Program 30 years ago. "Although Head Start is known for its attention to parents," writes Ellen Frede of Trenton State College, "in most programs, home visits are made only a few times per year (not weekly), and the visits are not conducted by the child's classroom staff."[193]

"Since its inception in 1965, [Head Start] has sought to combine comprehensive family support services with a quality preschool education program," writes Hirokazu Yoshikawa of New York University. "But the family support components of the program are in need of improvement. More than one-third of programs in 1993 had social service worker caseloads of more than 250."[194] That is seven times the ratio (35:1) recommended in 1993 by a federal advisory commission on Head Start.

Scientific studies in the 1970s and '80s showed that the short-term gains achieved by Head Start children did not sustain themselves over time – typically disappearing during the elementary school years. Moreover, no scientifically valid studies have been conducted in recent years to verify that even these short-term gains are still being produced in Head Start. In 1997 the General Accounting Office, an investigative arm of the U.S. Congress, reviewed the scientific research on Head Start and concluded that "Findings from early studies...do not conclusively establish the impact of the current Head Start program because today's program differs from that of the late 1960s and early 1970s.... Later studies offered to support Head Start's impact do not provide enough evidence to conclude that current Head Start is effective."[195]

The Drug Abuse Resistance Program (D.A.R.E.) curriculum is taught by police officers to 5th and 6th grade students in 80 percent of all school districts nationwide, at a cumulative cost of some $750 million per year. Repeated evaluations have found that the core D.A.R.E. curriculum produces no effect on long-term substance abuse.

School-Based Prevention.

School-based violence and substance-abuse prevention has been a major growth industry in the United States in recent years. The U.S. Department of Education allocates $500 million each year to communities to promote Safe and Drug Free Schools. Particularly in the wake of Columbine and other highly publicized school violence episodes of recent years, state education agencies and local school boards are also contributing funds for school-based prevention programming. In the majority of cases, however, the programs selected by schools lack evidence of effectiveness and are implemented without strong training or technical support. The Drug Abuse Resistance Program (D.A.R.E.) curriculum is taught by police officers to 5th and

6th grade students in 80 percent of all school districts nationwide, at a cumulative cost of some $750 million per year.[196] Repeated evaluations have found that the core D.A.R.E. curriculum produces no effect on long-term substance abuse.[197]

The most common activity funded under the Safe and Drug Free Schools Act are Student Assistance Programs, which provide individual, group and peer counseling to high-risk students. These counseling programs consume roughly half of the $500 million allocated by the federal government each year, but a recent review of this model revealed that evaluation studies are "universally absent."[198] The impact of federal school-based prevention funds is further hampered by a lack of targeting: currently 97 percent of all school districts nationwide receive Safe and Drug Free Schools grant funds, and the average funding per pupil is just $6-8 per year – not nearly enough to support stable and effective prevention programming.[199]

In 1997, a federally-funded study of school-based prevention programming in 19 school districts found that "few districts seem to know about or consider research findings when planning their prevention programs" and "few districts also conducted formal program evaluations to assess their program's effectiveness and identify areas in need of improvement... Further, only a few of those districts [that did conduct evaluations] used the results of the evaluations to improve their programs."[200] Looking specifically at drug abuse prevention, the study found that "prevention approaches that have been shown to be effective are not widely used, while approaches that have not shown effectiveness or have not been evaluated properly are the most common approaches currently in use."[201]

Rectifying these problems, the study's authors found, will require an information campaign to alert educators about what works and doesn't work, training for teachers, and ongoing expert assistance for schools. The study found that in order to be successful, school-based prevention efforts "need to be **stable** (in place for a long period of time, with continuity of staff, planning and leadership) and **extensive** (have multiple components that target both the general student population as well as high-risk students...)."[202] Without the guidance and sufficient financial support to implement stable, extensive, and effective prevention programs, the study concluded, "schools may opt instead for programs they can afford or programs that can be most easily implemented, given the myriad other demands on schools to respond to other social problems."[203]

In 1997, a federally-funded study of school-based prevention programming in 19 school districts found that "few districts seem to know about or consider research findings when planning their prevention programs" and "few districts also conducted formal program evaluations to assess their program's effectiveness and identify areas in need of improvement... Further, only a few of those districts [that did conduct evaluations] used the results of the evaluations to improve their programs."

Effective Child Welfare.

When the Child Welfare League of America examined the problem of child abuse and neglect among children in Sacramento, California in 1994, it found that 1,026 (1.4 percent) of the 75,000 children in the County ages 9-12 had been referred to the child welfare system at least once

"Research and experience demonstrate that the services available in the juvenile justice system to alleviate [mental health] problems are entirely inadequate."

for an investigation of child mistreatment. These one thousand children, however, accounted for half of all arrests among this age group. In other words, the children reported abused or neglected were 67 times more likely to be arrested between the ages of 9 and 12 than other children.[204]

In Massachusetts, a January 2000 study by the Citizens for Juvenile Justice found that 54 percent of all delinquent youth in the care of the state's juvenile corrections agency are clients of the Massachusetts Department of Social Services, which oversees child welfare services. Among youth designated by a Massachusetts juvenile court as "Children in Need of Supervision" due to running away from home, continually disobeying their guardians, truancy, or chronic misbehavior in school, 54 percent were referred to adult or juvenile court within three years, the study found, "clearly indicating a failure of the statute and system to prevent delinquency."[205]

Nationwide, the need to bolster and reform child welfare systems has grown increasingly apparent in recent years. "Child advocates, researchers, and other critics of the child welfare system have long contended that the system is underfunded, that caseload sizes exceed professional guidelines for effective practice, and that increased service demand is exacerbating an already difficult situation," reported the Urban Institute in 1999. Despite increasing caseloads, however, more than 30 states froze or cut child welfare spending during the early 1990s. Lack of needed support services also handicaps efforts to serve families effectively. "Child welfare staff in almost every state we visited reported that families often face long waiting lists for mental health services (especially for children) and substance abuse treatment," the Urban Institute reported.[206]

Intervening With Behaviorally Troubled Children.

Most juvenile crime is committed by a handful of serious and chronic offenders. These offenders almost always demonstrate behavior problems early in life, and prevention scholars have developed effective intervention strategies to arrest the progression of negative behaviors in children who demonstrate conduct problems. However, the best of these strategies are not in widespread use nationwide. Despite 15 years of research demonstrating powerful results for conduct-disordered children, for instance, Dr. Carolyn Webster-Stratton's "Incredible Years" is widely replicated only in Delaware, which funded expansion of the model to an additional 10 sites for each of the past years. In 1999, Webster-Stratton sold 250 copies of the curriculum and trained 300-500 proffesionals on how to implement the model. But systematic support for widespread replication remains unavailable.[207]

Likewise, despite widespread mental illness among the delinquency population, the nation's community mental health agencies are often unable or unwilling to serve juvenile justice youth – or they provide care lacking the intensity and quality required. As Shay Bilchik, former Administrator of the federal Office of Juvenile Justice and Delinquency Prevention, wrote in 1998. "Research and experience demonstrate that the services available in the juvenile justice system to alleviate these problems are entirely inadequate."[208]

The large majority of funds for mental health treatment of children and youth are spent for out-of-home treatment: one-half of all mental health dollars for minors pay for inpatient hospitalization, and another 25 percent is spent to place youth into residential facilities such as therapeutic treatment centers and group homes also costing hundreds of dollars per day.[209] Even with their high costs, however, hospitalization and other out-of-home treatments have not proven highly effective in resolving the mental health problems of youth.

In 1999, U.S. Surgeon General David Satcher concluded that "Inpatient care consumes about half of child mental health resources, based on the latest estimate available, but it is the clinical intervention with the weakest research support." Likewise, Satcher also raised concerns about overreliance on residential treatment centers (RTC's): "In the past, admission to an RTC has been justified on the basis of community protection, child protection, and benefits of residential treatment per se. However, none of these justifications have stood up to research scrutiny. In particular, youth who display seriously violent and aggressive behavior do not appear to improve in such settings."[210] In a six-state study of children in publicly funded residential treatment centers, 75 percent of youth treated at an RTC were either readmitted to a mental health facility (about 45 percent) or incarcerated in a correctional setting (about 30 percent) within seven years.[211]

Few local mental health agencies devote adequate resources to home-based treatment of troubled youth. Moreover, many expert critics complain that the services provided by mental health agencies are not well-suited to the needs of many high-risk adolescents. Thomas Sexton, a University of Nevada-Las Vegas professor who oversees the replication of the Functional Family Therapy model nationwide, faults mental health professionals for not working harder to engage high-risk youth and families in the therapy process. "Psychologists have had a great deal for a long time," Sexton says. "If the patient does not get engaged, then he's treatment resistant and not ready to participate. So it's not the therapist's responsibility. What FFT said is that because we're working with a treatment-resistant population, the initial engagement and motivation is the therapist's business."[212] Only a handful of mental health departments nationwide offer Multisystemic Therapy, Functional Family Therapy, or any of the other intensive, family-focused intervention strategies that have demonstrated success in producing sustainable change in troubled youth.

RECOMMENDATIONS:

Meeting the Juvenile Crime Challenge

Based on the glaring gaps that exist between proven best practices and the common practices in states and communities across the nation, the broad outlines of a safe and effective plan for improving America's approach to youth crime prevention are not difficult to discern:

- Provide research-proven treatment and services for young children with behavioral problems and their families.
- Use objective screening criteria to identify youthful offenders at highest risk to re-offend, and work intensively with them.
- Deliver community-based, family-focused treatment for delinquent youth who pose no risk to the community.
- Reduce reliance on correctional training schools and other out-of-home placements for delinquent youth who do not endanger public safety.
- Offer alternatives-to-detention for non-dangerous juvenile offenders awaiting trial.
- Implement "graduated sanctions," including treatment and youth development services, to ensure appropriate, predictable, and proportionate responses whenever delinquent youth commit additional crimes or violate probation.
- Correct justice system biases that perpetuate unequal access to treatment and services as well as disproportionate confinement of minority youth.
- Coordinate services among agencies – juvenile justice, education, mental health and child welfare – that share responsibility for troubled youth.
- Recruit local volunteers and engage community-based organizations to work directly with high-risk and delinquent youth.
- Develop alternative programs like drug courts, teen courts, family-group conferencing, and victim-offender mediation to hold young offenders accountable while connecting them to positive resources in their communities.
- Make quality aftercare a core component of juvenile corrections programs to help youthful offenders make a successful transition back into the community following their confinement.
- Support intensive early childhood intervention programs to promote the healthy development of infants and toddlers in high-risk families.
- Implement effective school-based prevention models.
- Mobilize the entire community to plan and implement comprehensive youth crime prevention strategies that involve families, schools, and neighborhoods.

Among knowledgeable experts, these approaches are not controversial. Solid research proves they work. They do not cost vast sums of money to implement, particularly compared to the money we now spend to commit ever-increasing numbers of young people to ineffective correctional programs at $40,000 to $50,000 per year.

Why then aren't these common sense innovations standard practice throughout our nation? University of South Carolina prevention scholar Gary Melton addressed this question in a 1997 essay: "Why wouldn't policy makers, policy administrators, and third-party payers rush to adopt service models that – in contrast to the services that are now widely available – are inexpensive, carefully and positively evaluated, easy to understand, and consistent with long-established values of respect for family integrity and personal liberty and privacy? If innovation is cheaper but more effective than current practices, why wouldn't it be quickly and widely adopted?"

"The nearly universal failure to adopt innovative service models as standard practice," Melton concluded, "reflects intrinsic but often tractable obstacles to reform."[213] Indeed, to capture the opportunities for reform, states and communities will have to overcome deep-rooted obstacles. Many state and local policymakers lack information about effective practices. Many agencies have limited capacity to plan and develop new programs effectively, and many lack start-up funding to support the spread of promising practices. Meanwhile, the political environment surrounding youth crime remains highly charged – exacerbating the tendency of public leaders to avoid risks and shun the kind of wrenching operational changes that would be required of professionals and agencies to implement many reforms.

For understandable reasons, then, the deck is now stacked against reforms urgently needed to hold down youth crime rates in the years to come. What will it take to overcome these obstacles and begin building positive momentum for progress against adolescent crime?

While the process will be long and complex, the first step is straightforward: We must elevate the debate over youth crime by rejecting the simplistic formulation of "adult time for adult crime" and dismissing proposals to disband juvenile courts or further erode their jurisdiction. Overwhelming evidence proves that transferring youth to adult courts exacerbates the criminality of those transferred and fails to deter crime among other youth. Powerful analysis demonstrates that ***measured punishments, high-quality treatment services, community-based youth development programming, and freedom from a criminal record are far more effective in turning delinquent youth away from crime than criminal prosecution or incarceration with adult convicts.***

Hundreds of years after the introduction of Common Law, the United States led the world in 1899 by creating the first court system in history specifically for young people. Today, separate juvenile justice systems operate in virtually every civilized nation on earth. With public concern over youth crime now high among the list of public concerns, ***America should not abandon this home-grown solution. Rather, we must re-embrace the juvenile justice ideal and dedicate ourselves to retooling and reforming our juvenile justice and delinquency prevention systems to meet the demands of a new century.***

Herein lies the more difficult challenge: strengthening and reshaping juvenile justice and delinquency prevention efforts nationwide to capitalize on our rapidly increasing knowledge of what works, take advantage of cost-effective new policy and program models, and discontinue programs and practices that have proven wasteful but remain commonplace. Specifically, five areas of strategic action offer the greatest promise:

1. End Over-Reliance on Corrections and Other Out-of-Home Placements

In most states, local juvenile courts face a strong financial incentive to commit troubled youth to corrections facilities rather than treat them locally. Juvenile corrections are typically a state function, often available at little or no cost to the local jurisdiction committing the offender. Likewise, most of the costs for placing youth into group homes and residential treatment centers are typically reimbursed with federal, state, or private insurance funds. By contrast, the costs to retain youth at home and provide community-based treatment fall entirely on the locality in most states. Thus, even if commitment to corrections would be less effective for an individual young person than intensive community-based treatment, even if it costs taxpayers many times more money, committing a young offender to corrections or to another out-of-home placement is often the only affordable option for local governments. In fact, lacking knowledge about the benefits of innovative home-based treatments and funding to set up these programs even if they do know, few localities have developed intensive community-based program options for their delinquent young people.

To reverse this counterproductive dynamic, ***states should revise their funding formulas to reward localities for serving youth in their homes and communities whenever possible. Localities should be required to pay a share of the costs of care for youth confined in state correctional facilities – except for the management of clearly dangerous, violent offenders in need of incapacitation.*** When Ohio tested a financing reform of this type in 1994, the new financial incentives led to a 43 percent drop in institutional commitments in the eight counties involved in the pilot. Called Reclaim Ohio, this innovative policy has since been enacted statewide.[214] California created a new sliding scale funding formula in 1996 requiring localities to pay 75 percent of the costs when they commit low-level offenders to the state corrections agency and 50 percent of costs when they commit moderately serious offenders. The state continued to pay for virtually all costs to confine the most serious youthful offenders. The results of the new funding formula were immediate: within two years the admissions rate for less serious offenders declined by 41 percent.[215]

To reduce unnecessary placements of delinquents and otherwise-troubled youth to group homes and residential treatment centers, several states and cities have begun developing "systems of care" reforms that offer financial incentives for contracted service providers to minimize reliance on out-of-home placements. The only agency in the nation providing both Multisystemic Therapy and Multidimensional Treatment Foster Care is Youth Villages, a Tennessee-based nonprofit agency funded through that state's TennCare initiative. Its contract with TennCare requires Youth Villages to provide quality care to youth at risk for out-of-home placement due to emotional disturbances or other problems, and the contract pays the agency a flat fee for its services to any young person. Thus, Youth Villages is encouraged to deliver the most effective services possible at the lowest price to limit the time a young person must spend in expensive out-of-home placements.

2. Invest in Research-Based Interventions for Juvenile Offenders, as well as Research-Based Prevention

The advances produced by delinquency scholars and research scientists over the past two decades offer an opportunity to revolutionize America's approach to juvenile crime. In fact, the new evidence demands drastic change, because it demonstrates clearly that today's common practices are often ineffective and sometimes counterproductive. To effect the needed changes, ***the federal government should invest heavily in the replication and further refinement of proven strategies, and in continuing research efforts to develop even better strategies for quelling delinquent conduct among troubled youth.***

In 1998, the federal government funded the University of Colorado's Center for the Study and Prevention of Violence to support local replication of eight proven violence prevention or treatment program models (including Multisystemic Therapy, Functional Family Therapy, and Multidimensional Treatment Foster Care). The program is a step in the right direction, but only a baby step: total funding for the four-year project was only $4 million. The project is limited to just 50 sites nationwide, and the funds support only training and consulting support for these efforts. Start-up and operating funds must come from the localities themselves. Given the serious barriers to innovation and reform in states and localities, ***the federal government should provide direct funding for replication of proven programs – including funds for training and technical assistance and matching funds for implementation. Both process and outcome evaluation should be required for all funded projects***.

The federal government should also sharpen the focus of its delinquency prevention [and substance abuse] prevention efforts. School-based prevention efforts tend to produce lasting benefits only when they are multi-dimensional – shifting the entire school climate rather than "teaching" prevention through an off-the-shelf, add-on curriculum. Educators clearly face a daunting challenge to make prevention work. Considering the evidence that many existing prevention programs yield no benefits, it makes little sense to continue funding school-based efforts without ensuring that the programs employed are supported by research and subject to meaningful outcome evaluation. In 1997, the U.S. Department of Education added requirements to the $500 million Safe and Drug Free Schools program requiring that states and localities measure results of programs funded with federal funds and select program strategies with some evidence of effectiveness. Another small first step in the right direction.

To foster local success in implementing effective programs, ***the federal government should also invest funds to build local capacity to implement effective multi-disciplinary intervention programs.*** Congress should invest in "technology transfer" to support replication of best practices in delinquency prevention and behavior change, and to provide ongoing training opportunities for juvenile justice and mental health professionals. These efforts should include both funding for researchers to prepare training and implementation manuals to guide replication efforts, and funding for state-level prevention and intervention specialists to work in local communities to heighten awareness of best practices and support replication of proven programs and strategies.

Finally, ***the federal government should coordinate and significantly intensify research and development into what works*** – including development and validation of new models; continued research into the causes, correlates and developmental pathways; and follow-up studies of effective models to determine when they work, how, for whom, and under what circumstances. To help bridge the continuing gap between academic researchers and local program practitioners, ***the federal government should provide funding (or set aside a portion of existing program funds) to support partnerships involving university-based prevention scholars in the implementation and evaluation of research-driven programs for high-risk children and families in juvenile courts, public schools, and community-based settings***.

3. Measure Results, Fund What Works, and Cut Funds to What Doesn't Work

Substantive information about programs, services, budgets and especially outcomes is hard to come by in most juvenile justice agencies. This scarcity of hard facts presents both a crucial problem today and an opportunity to spur meaningful reforms in the future. Available evidence shows that many current juvenile justice and delinquency prevention efforts are ineffective, and that some are actually counterproductive. Thus, measuring results is critical.

Here the role of the federal government is paramount. As renowned UCLA criminologist James Q. Wilson wrote in 1996, "[Washington's key role in crime policy] ought to be to do the one thing local authorities cannot and will not do on their own.... The federal government has a unique opportunity to be the research and development arm for law enforcement.... We know that states and counties differ in how they handle juveniles, but we have almost no idea as to whether those differences make a difference in crime rates."[216]

Over the past decade, the federal Office of Juvenile Justice and Delinquency Prevention has done excellent work on two elements of its mission: supporting valuable primary and applied research studies into the causes and correlates of crime, and disseminating a "Comprehensive Strategy" for juvenile crime control which has become a guiding light for state and local reform efforts throughout the nation. However, OJJDP has not issued meaningful evaluation requirements for the hundreds of millions of dollars it provides to states and localities in formula funds and block grants. ***Given the federal government's key role in research and development, and given its small percentage of the nation's overall juvenile justice and delinquency prevention budgets, developing new knowledge must be a core goal for all federal spending in these areas.*** Thus, meaningful and standardized process and outcome information should be required from all federal grantees.

State leadership is also critical for data collection and program evaluation, yet it is often absent. Roughly half of all states have no data on the success and failure rates of state juvenile corrections programs. Some states, notably California, maintain no data on juvenile court caseloads or outcomes on a statewide basis. Florida, however, is demonstrating the potential of meaningful research and evaluation as a tool to guide continual improvement of state policies and programs. Florida's Department of Juvenile Justice has developed a standardized format to measure the effectiveness of every correctional program statewide, both residential and non-residential. Florida publishes annual reports detailing the success rates of every program as well as the "expected success rates" based on the characteristics of young people enrolled in the program.[217] On the local level, Philadelphia has also developed a management information system to measure the success of all programs serving juvenile offenders, and San Francisco is in the process of developing a similar tool.

Such program outcome databases should be created by states and cities throughout the nation. Not only do they offer a tool for policymakers to identify what is working and shift funds accordingly, they also represent a necessary tool to support fundamental reforms. Given the highly politicized tone of most policy debates on juvenile crime, calls for reasoned reform are too often drowned out by shrill voices and entrenched interests. If innovative program models are consistently compared to existing business-as-usual programs head-to-head, their superiority will become evident and momentum for reform is likely to build. Without such head-to-head comparisons, reform will be less likely.

4. Engage Community Partners

Two of the characteristic traits of youth who fall into delinquent lifestyles are a lack of attachment to caring adults and a lack of involvement in school and other positive, pro-social activities in their communities – an afterschool program, a job, church, community service. "Disconnected" youth comprise the lion's share of the delinquency population. In many or most localities, juvenile courts and juvenile justice agencies also suffer from a "disconnection" problem. While they routinely refer youth to service providers in their communities, many juvenile courts have not formed strong working partnerships either with partner agencies, community organizations, or local citizens to help fill in the missing pieces in delinquent youths' lives.

Re-connecting youth to their communities through innovative "restorative justice" initiatives like family-group conferences, teen courts, drug courts, and youth aid panels offers a promising and important strategy for revitalizing juvenile justice. State and local juvenile justice authorities should step up their efforts to apply these models. Unlike most juvenile courts, these alternative programs provide intensive and ongoing individualized attention to juvenile offenders before they commit serious crimes. By providing both treatment services to those in need and requiring offenders to take responsibility for their delinquent acts, these strategies turn the court process into an opportunity to re-connect youth rather than further alienating them from mainstream society.

In these and all other efforts, ***juvenile courts and probation agencies should be encouraged or even required to strengthen partnerships with community residents and organizations.*** By placing young people with indigenous community organizations and concerned individuals, juvenile courts can create opportunities for youth to re-connect with positive influences and insulate themselves from negative peers who might otherwise drag them back into delinquent behaviors. Community-based organizations are ideally suited to provide many of important services and programs for court-involved youth – alternatives to detention, case-advocacy, intensive supervision and wrap-around – that have proven promising as complements to probation supervision and alternatives to out-of-home placement. Moreover, these ties to community resources can benefit young people long after their juvenile justice involvement has concluded. In order to maximize these potential contributions, ***local courts and probation departments should consider setting aside a percentage of their budgets for contracts with community-based service providers. They should also make every effort to recruit and utilize community volunteers to engage and work with delinquent youth.***

A second critical area for improving connections is to enhance collaboration with other government agencies concerned with high-risk youth. Here, action should be undertaken at all levels of government. ***States should support "systems of care" reforms that reward and support multi-agency partnerships to provide case-management and intervention treatment services for delinquent youth,*** as well as youth under the supervision of the child welfare system and those suffering with severe emotional disturbances. ***At the local level, multi-agency teams should be established to jointly assess and oversee treatment of high-risk youth involved in child welfare, special education, juvenile justice, and mental health systems.*** Finally, to encourage and enhance these systems integration efforts, ***the federal government should expand funding for community mental health services to children with severe emotional disturbances.***

5. Mobilize Whole Communities to Study, Plan and Implement Comprehensive Strategies for Combatting Youth Crime

Timely outcome data on programs is one potential lever for reform. A second invaluable lever for change is a cadre of engaged and informed leaders at the local level. Only when a broad-based group of community leaders examines the specific trends, problems, assets, and risk factors present in a locality can they effectively target their limited resources for juvenile justice and delinquency prevention. Only when a broad array of leaders – representing all agencies concerned with youth and with law enforcement, as well as all segments of the local community – becomes informed and active in addressing delinquency issues comprehensively can bureaucratic resistance be overcome.

Since 1994, the Office of Juvenile Justice and Delinquency Prevention has provided funds for communities to undertake comprehensive planning. Employing a strategy called "Communities That Care," OJJDP has funded more than 600 communities to undertake six-step processes for promoting positive youth development and preventing delinquency and related problem behaviors such as substance abuse, teen pregnancy, and school failure. The six Communities that Care phases include engaging key constituents and leaders to form a local Prevention Policy Board; training local leaders on delinquency prevention issues and model programs and strategies; collecting extensive data on risks, problems and resources in the community; developing comprehensive local plans for preventing and responding effectively to delinquency; implementing these comprehensive plans; and monitoring progress toward achieving clear goals and revising strategies to maximize success.

Several states have also adopted Communities That Care as a core strategy for attacking youth crime, and the early results appear to be positive. An analysis by the non-partisan General Accounting Office in Washington found that 90 percent of communities participating in the process implemented two or more evidence-based delinquency prevention programs, and three-fourths developed multiple approaches to addressing the risk factors identified in their jurisdictions. Participating communities have also been effective in raising state and local resources to support investment in their delinquency prevention plans.[218]

Despite these results, some proposals now pending in Congress call for the elimination of federal funding for comprehensive community planning and mobilization. ***Congress should reject these proposals and instead continue and expand funding for comprehensive community analysis, planning, and mobilization. States should emulate Kansas' example by requiring local jurisdictions to create local policy boards and to develop and submit community plans as a condition for receiving state funds and federal pass-through funds for juvenile justice and delinquency prevention programming.*** Finally, whether or not they are subject to state planning mandates or receive federal planning funds, ***communities should mobilize local leaders and residents to participate in intensive analysis, planning, and program development*** in order to mount integrated and comprehensive campaigns to meet the challenges of youth crime and seize the opportunities created by new knowledge about what works.

Rising to the Juvenile Justice Challenge.

The actions recommended above are only a beginning – the starting point for a long, difficult but urgently-needed campaign to reconstitute our nation's juvenile justice and delinquency prevention systems and make them conform to our growing knowledge of what works.

To make a difference at the state and community levels, this list will have to be fleshed out with specific proposals for reforming juvenile detention practices, establishing effective prevention programs, developing and implementing graduated sanctions and community-based programming for youthful offenders, treating conduct disorders, and replacing training schools with smaller, more community-based correctional programs. Indeed, the specific challenges in juvenile justice and delinquency reform are many.

These recommendations omit the fundamental rights violations that continue to plague juvenile justice and demand redress. Disproportionate treatment of minority youth remains pervasive and undermines both the integrity and the effectiveness of juvenile justice. Continuing problems with maltreatment of juvenile correctional inmates and substandard conditions of confinement are a blight on our society's honor, and a significant barrier to successful rehabilitation of juvenile offenders.

Finally, the recommendations above do not mention the crucial pre-requisite for success in juvenile justice: that is to elevate the quality of our nation's discourse on the subject of juvenile crime. Only when we reject alarmist rhetoric about juvenile "superpredators," only when we engage in more balanced, rational, and productive discussions can an effective response to juvenile crime emerge.

More and more, citizens and political leaders have grown quick to condemn the values and conduct of young people. "Impetuous," we call them, "brash, reckless, unable to think through consequences..." Yet in recent years these very qualities have crept into Adult America's response to youth and youth crime.

Americans are right to view youth crime as a major concern for our society. If we are willing to roll up our sleeves and get to work, effective solutions are now available. The time has come for communities and political leaders to rise to this challenge.

ENDNOTES

1. Henggeler, S.W., Melton, G.B., & Smith, L.A., "Family Preservation Using Multisystemic Therapy: An Effective Alternative to Incarcerating Serious Juvenile Offenders," *Journal of Consulting and Clinical Psychology*, vol. 60, 1992, pp. 953-961, cited in *Blueprints for Violence Prevention Book Six: Multisystemic Therapy* (Boulder, CO: Center for the Study and Prevention of Violence, 1998).
2. Borduin, C.M., Mann, B.J., Cone, L.T., Henggeler, S.W., Fucci, B.R., Blaske, D.M.. & Williams, R.A., "Multisystemic Treatment of Serious Juvenile Offenders: Long-Term Prevention of Criminality and Violence," *Journal of Consulting and Clinical Psychology*, vol. 63, no. 4, 1995, pp. 569-578.
3. Alexander, J.F. & Parsons, B.V., "Short Term Behavioral Intervention With Delinquent Families: Impact on Family Process and Recidivism," *Journal of Abnormal Psychology*, vol. 81, 1973, pp. 219-225, cited in *Blueprints for Violence Prevention Book Three: Functional Family Therapy* (Boulder, CO: Center for the Study and Prevention of Violence, 1998).
4. Barton, C., Alexander, J.F., Waldron, H., Turner, C.W., & Warburton, J., "Generalizing Treatment Effects of Functional Family Therapy: Three Replications," *American Journal of Family Therapy*, vol. 13, 1985, pp. 16-26, cited in *Blueprints for Violence Prevention Book Three: Functional Family Therapy*, ibid.
5. Cited in *Blueprints for Violence Prevention Book Three: Functional Family Therapy*, ibid.
6. Chamberlain, P., "Comparative evaluation of Specialized Foster Care for Seriously Delinquent Youths: A First Step," *Comparative Alternatives: International Journal of Family Care*, vol.2, 1990, p.21-36, cited in *Blueprints for Violence Prevention Book Eight: Multidimensional Treatment Foster Care* (Boulder, CO: Center for the Study and Prevention of Violence, 1998).
7. Chamberlain, P., & Reid, J.B., *Comparison of Two Community Alternatives to Incarceration for Juvenile Offenders*, manuscript submitted for publication, 1997, cited in *Blueprints for Violence Prevention Book Eight,* ibid.
8. Aos, S., Phipps, P., Barnoski, R., Lieb, R., *The Comparative Costs and Benefits of Programs to Reduce Crime: A Review of National Research Findings With Implications for Washington State*, Washington State Institute for Public Policy, May 1999, p.8.
9. Wolfgang, M.E., Figlio, R.M., & Sellin, T., *Delinquency in a Birth Cohort* (Chicago, IL: University of Chicago, 1972).
10. Tracy, P., Wolfgang, M.E., & Figlio, R.M., *Delinquency in Two Birth Cohorts*, Washington, DC: Office of Juvenile Justice and Delinquency Prevention, 1990), cited in Howell, J.C. (Ed.), *Guide for Implementing the Comprehensive Strategy for Serious, Violent, and Chronic Juvenile Offenders* (Washington, DC: Office of Juvenile Justice and Delinquency Prevention, 1995).
11. *Guide for Implementing*, ibid, p.2.
12. Elliott, D.S., "Serious and Violent Offenders: Onset, Developmental Course, and Termination" (The American Society of Criminology 1993 Presidential Address), reprinted in *Criminology*, vol.32, no.1, February 1994.
13. Tolan, P.H., Gorman-Smith, D., "Development of Serious and Violent Offending Careers," cited in Loeber, R., & Farrington, D.P. (Eds.) *Serious & Violent Juvenile Offenders: Risk Factors and Successful Interventions* (Thousand Oaks, CA: Sage Publications, 1998), p.81.
14. Steinberg, Lawrence, Director of John D. and Catherine T. MacArthur Foundation Research Network on Adolescent and Juvenile Violence, "Testimony Before the House Bi-Partisan Working Group on Youth Violence," September 15, 1999.
15. Ibid.

16. Zimring, F.E., "Toward a Jurisprudence of Youth Violence," in Tonry, M., & Moore, M.H. (Eds.), *Youth Violence: Crime and Justice A Review of Research, Volume 24* (Chicago, IL: University of Chicago Press, 1998), p.489.

17 Dishion, T.J., McCord, J., & Poulin, F., "When Interventions Harm: Peer Groups and Problem Behavior," *American Psychologist*, vol. 54, no. 9, September 1999, pp.755-764.

18 Moffit, T., *Juvenile Delinquency: Seed of a Career in Violent Crime, Just Sowing Wild Oats Or Both?* (Washington, DC: Federation of Behavioral, Psychological and Cognitive Sciences, 1994).

19. Szapocznik, J., and Williams, R.A., "Brief Strategic Family Therapy: Twenty-Five Years of Interplay Among Theory, Research and Practice In Adolescent Behavior Problems and Drug Abuse," *Clinical Child and Family Psychology Review*, in press.

20. Santiseban, D.A., & Szapocznik, J., Perez-Vidal, A., Kurtines, W.M., Coatsworth, J.D., & LaPierre, A., *The Efficacy of Brief Strategic/Structural Family Therapy in Modifying Behavior Problems and an Exploration of the Role That Family Functioning Plays in Behavior Change*, manuscript in preparation, University of Miami, Center of Family Studies, cited in Szapocznik & Williams, ibid.

21. Schmidt, S.E., Liddle, H.A., & Dakof, G.A., "Changes in Parenting Practices and Adolescent Drug Abuse During Multidimensional Family Therapy," *Journal of Family Psychology*, vol. 10, no.1, 1996, pp.12-27.

22. Cited in Liddle, H.A., & Dakof, G.A., "Family-Based Treatment for Adolescent Drug Use: State of the Science," in Rahdert, E., & Czechowicz, (Eds.), *Adolescent Drug Abuse: Clinical Assessment and Therapeutic Interventions (NIDA Research Monograph no. 156, NIH Publication No. 95-3908)*, 1995, p.229, and Liddle, H.A., Dakof, G.A., Diamond, G., Barrett, K., & Tejeda, M., "Multidimensional Family Treatment of Adolescent Substance Abuse," unpublished paper, 1998.

23. Goldman, S.K., & Faw, L., "Three Wraparound Models as Promising Approaches," in Burns, B.J., & Goldman, S.K. (Eds.), *Promising Practices in Wraparound for Children With Serious Emotional Disturbances and Their Families – Systems of Care: Promising Practices in Children's Mental Health, 1998 Series, Volume IV* (Washington, DC: Center for Effective Collaboration and Practice, American Institutes for Research, 1999), pp.17-33.

24. Satcher, D.A., *Mental Health: A Report of the Surgeon General* (Rockville, MD: U.S. Department of Health and Human Services, Substance Abuse and Mental Health Services Administration, Center for Mental Health Services, National Institutes of Health, National Institute of Mental Health, 1999), p.185.

25. Data provided by Eric Seybold, Program Evaluator, Milwaukee County Health Division, Child & Adolescent Services Branch, April 2000.

26. Cited in *Guide for Implementing*, supra, n.10, pp.150-151.

27. Schumacher, M., & Kurz, G.A., *The 8% Solution: Preventing Serious, Repeat Juvenile Crime* (Thousand Oaks, CA: Sage Publications, 2000), p.66.

28. Data provided by the Orange County Probation Department, February 2000.

29. Boyle, P., "In New Courts, Kids on Drugs Get the Treatment," *Youth Today*, vol 9, no.3, April 2000, p.1.

30. Butts, J., Hoffman, D., & Buck, J., *Teen Courts in the United States: A Profile of Current Programs*, OJJDP Fact Sheet #118 (Washington, DC: Office of Juvenile Justice and Delinquency Prevention, October 1999).

31. Several juvenile gun court initiatives are described in *Promising Strategies to Reduce Gun Violence* (Washington, DC: Office of Juvenile Justice and Delinquency Prevention, 1999).

32. Phone interview with Michael Cleary, Assistant District Attorney, April 2000, and DiIulio, J.J., & Palubinsky, B.Z., "How Philadelphia Salvages Teen Criminals," *City Journal*, Summer 1997.

33. Bazemore, G, & Terry, W.C., "Developing Delinquent Youths: A Reintegrative Model for Rehabilitation and a New Role for the Juvenile Justice System," *Child Welfare*, vol. 74, no.5, 1997, pp.665-716.

34. Cleary, and DiIulio & Palubinsky, supra, n.32.

35. Harrell, A., *Drug Courts and the Role of Graduated Sanctions*, Summary Presentation (Washington, DC: Office of Juvenile Justice and Delinquency Prevention, 1998).
36. *Juvenile Detention Alternatives Initiative: An Experiment in Reform*, downloaded from the website of the Annie E. Casey Foundation, www.aecf.org/initiatives/juvenile/exper.htm.
37. Program information provided by Ms. Jody Schwarz, Executive Director, Center on Juvenile and Criminal Justice, April, 2000.
38. Shelden, R.G., *Detention Diversion Advocacy: An Evaluation* (Washington, DC: Office of Juvenile Justice and Delinqency Prevention, September 1999).
39. For a review of this research, see Krisberg, B., *The Impact of the Justice System on Serious, Violent, and Chronic Juvenile Offenders* (San Francisco: National Council on Crime and Delinquency, 1997).
40. Cited in *Guide for Implementing*, supra, n.10, pp. 155-156.
41. *AMI 1999 Recidivism Study* (Tampa, FL: Associated Marine Institutes, 1999).
42. Ms. Judy Briscoe, Texas Youth Commission, interview with the author, February 2000.
43. *1999 Review of Agency Effectiveness* (Austin, TX: Texas Youth Commission, 1999).
44. Cited in *Guide for Implementing*, supra, n.10, p.155.
45. Lally, J.R., Mangione, P.L., & Honig, A.S., "The Syracuse Family Development Research Program: Long-Range Impact of an Early Intervention With Low-Income Children and Their Families," in *Parent Education as Early Childhood Intervention: Emerging Directions in Theory, Research and Practice*, D.R. Powell (Ed.) (Norwood, NJ: Ablex Publishing Corp., 1988).
46. Schweinhart, L.J., Barnes, H.V., & Weikart, D.V., *Significant Benefits: The High/Scope Perry Preschool Study Through Age 27* (Ypsilanti, MI: High/Scope Press, 1993).
47. Cited in Greenberg, M.T., Domitrovich, C., & Bumbarger, B., *Preventing Mental Disorders in School-age Children: A Review of the Effectiveness of Prevention Programs*, Prevention Research Center for the Promotion of Human Development, Pennsylvania State University, July 1999.
48. Cited in *Blueprints for Violence Prevention Book Nine: Bullying Prevention Program* (Boulder, CO: Center for the Study and Prevention of Violence, 1998).
49. Cited in Greenberg et al., supra n.47.
50. Aber, J.A., Brown, J.L., & Henrich, C.C., *Teaching Conflict Resolution: An Effective School-Based Approach to Violence Prevention* (New York: National Center for Children in Poverty, 1999).
51. Cited in Flannery, D.J., *School Violence: Risk, Preventive Intervention, and Policy* (New York: ERIC Clearinghouse in Urban Education, December 1997).
52. Cited in Catalano, R.F., Berglund, M., Ryan, J.A.M., Lonczak, H.S., Hawkins, J.D., *Positive Youth Development in the United States: Research Findings on Evaluations of Positive Youth Development Programs* (Seattle: Social Development Research Group, 1998).
53. Cited in *Guide for Implementing*, supra n.10, pp.93-94.
54. Schinke, P.P., Orlandi, M.A., & Cole, K.C., "Boys & Girls Clubs in Public Housing Developments: Prevention Services for Youth at Risk," *Journal of Community Psychology*, OSAP Special Issue, 1992.
55. Tierney, J.P., Grossman, J.B., with Resch, N.L., *Making a Difference: An Impact Study of Big Brothers Big Sisters* (Philadelphia, PA: Public/Private Ventures, Inc., 1995).
56. Hahn, A., with Leavitt, T. and Aaron, P., *Evaluation of the Quantum Opportunities Program (QOP): Did the Program Work?* (Waltham, MA:Center for Human Resources, Brandeis University, June 1994).
57. Tierney, J., & Lozillon, A., *Critical Issues Facing Philadelphia's Neighborhoods: Violence Reduction* (Philadelphia, PA: Public/Private Ventures, n.d.).

58. *Youth Violence: A Community-Based Response — One City's Success* (Washington, DC: U.S. Department of Justice, September 1996).
59. *Six Safer Cities: On the Crest of the Crime Prevention Wave* (Washington, DC: National Crime Prevention Council, 1999), p.3.
60. Cited in *False Images: The News Media and Juvenile Crime (1997 Annual Report)* (Washington, DC: Coalition for Juvenile Justice, 1997), p.11.
61. Dorfman, L., Woodruff, K., Chavez, V., & Wallack, L., "Youth and Violence on Local Television News," *American Journal of Public Health*, vol. 87, no.8, August1997, pp.1311-1316.
62. Cited in *False Images*, supra, n. 60, pp.13-14.
63. Schiraldi, V., "Hyping Juvenile Crime: A Media Staple," *Christian Science Monitor*, November 6, 1997.
64. Elikann, Peter, *Superpredators: The Demonization of Our Children By the Law* (New York: Insight Books, 1999), p.57.
65. Males, M., "Wild in Deceit: Why 'Teen Violence' is Poverty Violence in Disguise ," *EXTRA!* , March/April 1996, pp. 7-9.
66. Schiraldi, Vincent, "Juvenile Crime Is Decreasing—It's Media Coverage That's Soaring," *Los Angeles Times*, November 23, 1999.
67. *Fear of Crime and Related Perceptions in Florida 1998 (Research Digest Issue #2000_A)*, Florida Department of Juvenile Justice, Bureau of Data and Research, 2000.
68. Schiraldi, *Los Angeles Times*, supra, n. 9.
69. Data cited in Brooks, K, Schiraldi, V., & Ziedenberg, J., *School House Hype: Two Years Later* (Washington, DC: Justice Policy Institute, 2000), and Donohue, E., Schiraldi, V., & Ziedenberg, J., *School House Hype: School shootings and the real risks kids face in America* (Washington, DC: Justice Policy Institute, July 1998).
70. *Juvenile Offenders and Victims: 1999 National Report* (Pittsburgh, PA: National Center for Juvenile Justice, 1999), p.134.
71. Cook, P.J., & Laub, J.H., "The Unprecedented Epidemic in Youth Violence," in Tonry, M., & Moore, M.H. (Eds.), *Youth Violence: Crime and Justice, A Review of Research,* Volume 24 (Chicago, IL: University of Chicago Press, 1998), pp.27-64.
72. Ibid, pp.52-53.
73. Thornberry, T.P., "Membership in Youth Gangs and Involvement in Serious and Violent Offending," in Loeber & Farrington, *Serious & Violent Juvenile Offenders*, p.148.
74. *Juvenile Offenders and Victims*, supra, n.70, p.79.
75. Anderson, E., "The Social Ecology of Youth Violence," in Loeber & Farrington, *Serious & Violent Juvenile Offenders*, pp.65-104.
76. Cited in Gay, J., "Rebels With a Cause," *Boston Phoenix*, April 22-29, 1999.
77. Males, M., "Wild in Deceit," supra, n.65.
78. Males, M., *The Scapegoat Generation: America*'s *War on Adolescents* (Monroe, ME: Common Courage Press, 1996).
79. *Juvenile Offenders and Victims*, supra, n.70, p.51.
80. Cook & Laub, supra, n.71, pp.36-37.
81. Ziedenberg, J., & Schiraldi, V., *Runaway Juvenile Crime?: The Context of Juvenile Arrests in America* (Washington, DC: Justice Policy Institute, March 1998).
82. *Juvenile Offenders and Victims: 1999 National Report*, supra, n.70, p.113, and Snyder, H.N., *Juvenile Arrests 1998* (Washington, DC: Office of Juvenile Justice and Delinquency Prevention, 2000).

83. Males, "Wild in Deceit," supra, n.65.
84. Elikann, supra, n.64, p.26.
85. Males, M., & Macallair, *Dispelling the Myth: An Analysis of Youth and Adult Corrections Patterns in California Over the Past 20 Years* (Washington, DC: Justice Policy Institute, March 2000).
86. Federal Bureau of Investigation, *Uniform Crime Reports* (Violent Index Offense Arrest Rates By Age, 1970-1978).
87. *Juvenile Offenders and Victims*, supra, n.70, p.25.
88. Data provided by National Center for Juvenile Justice.
89. Cited in Garbarino, J., *Lost Boys: Why Our Sons Turn Violent and How We Can Save Them* (New York: Free Press, 1999), pp.233-234.
90. Torbet, P., Gable, R., Hurst, H., Montgomery, I., Szymanski, L., & Thomas, D., *State Responses to Serious and Violent Juvenile Crime* (Pittsburgh, PA: National Center for Juvenile Justice, 1996).
91. Torbet, P., & Szymanski, L., *State Legislative Responses to Juvenile Crime: 1996-97 Update* (Washington, DC: Office of Juvenile Justice and Delinquency Prevention, 1998).
92. Griffin, P., Torbet, P., Szymanski, L., *Trying Juveniles as Adults in Criminal Court: An Analysis of State Transfer Provisions* (Washington, DC: Office of Juvenile Justice and Delinquency Prevention, 1998).
93. Bishop, D, & Frazier C., "The Consequences of Waiver," in Fagan, J., & Zimring, F.E.,(Eds.) *The Changing Borders of Juvenile Justice: Transfer of Adolescents to the Criminal Court* (Chicago, IL: University of Chicago Press, forthcoming).
94. Unpublished data provided by Mr. Ted Tollett, Chief of the Bureau of Research and Data, Florida Department of Juvenile Justice, March 2000.
95. Butts, J.A., & Harrell, A.V., *Delinquents or Criminals: Policy Options for Young Offenders* (Washington, DC: Urban Institute, 1998), p.7.
96. Neff, J., "Juvenile Time Often Tougher Than Adult," *[Raleigh, NC] News & Observer*,
97. Ibid.
98. Myers, David L., *Excluding Violent Youths From Juvenile Court: The Effectiveness of Legislative Waiver* (Doctoral Dissertation, University of Maryland Department of Criminology, 1999), downloaded from http://www.preventingcrime.org, Chapter 8.
99. Data reported in Bishop & Frazier, supra n. 93.
100. Cited in Bishop & Frazier, ibid.
101. Podkopacz, M.R., & Feld, B.C., "The End of the Line: An Empirical Study of Judicial Waiver," *Journal of Criminal Law and Criminology*, vol.86, no.2, Winter 1986, pp.449-492.
102. Singer, S.I., & McDowall, D., "Criminalizing Delinquency: The Deterrent Effects of the New York Juvenile Offender Law," *Law and Society Review*, vol. 22, 1988, pp.521-535, cited in Myers, supra, n.98, Chapter 4.
103. Jensen, E.J., & Metsger, L.K., "A Test of the Deterrent Effect of Legislative Waiver on Violent Juvenile Crime," *Crime & Delinquency*, vol. 40, 1994, pp.96-104.
104. Strom, K.J., *Profile of State Prisoners Under Age 18, 1985-97* (Washington, DC: Bureau Of Justice Statistics, 2000).
105. *Juvenile Offenders and Victims*, supra, n.70, p.208.
106. Flaherty, Michael G., *An Assessment of the national incidence of juvenile suicide in adult jails, lockups, and juvenile detention centers* (Urbana_Champaign, IL: University of Illinois, 1980), cited in Ziedenberg, J., & Schiraldi, V., *The Risks Juveniles Face When They Are Incarcerated With Adults* (Washington, DC: Justice Policy Institute, 1997).

107. Fagan, Jeffrey, Martin Forst and T. Scott Vivona. "Youth In Prisons and Training Schools: Perceptions and Consequences of the Treatment_Custody Dichotomy." *Juvenile and Family Court*, no. 2, 1989., cited in Ziedenberg & Schiraldi, ibid.
108. Ibid.
109. Ibid.
110. Bishop & Frazier, supra, n.148.
111. Ibid.
112. *Juvenile Offenders and Victims*, supra, n.70, pp.179-180.
113. Ibid, p.181.
114. Ibid, p.209
115. Ibid, p.173.
116 .*Prosecuting Juveniles in Adult Court: An Assessment of Trends and Consequences* (Washington, DC: The Sentencing Project, undated), downloaded from http://www.sentencingproject.org/brief/juveniles.html, May 2000.
117. Bishop & Frazier, supra, n.93.
118. *Analysis of Propositions for Election: March 7, 2000*, (Sacramento, CA: Legislative Analyst's Office, November 1999).
119. See Zimring, "Toward a Jurisprudence of Youth Violence," supra, n.73, pp.485-493.
120. Ibid, pp.488-489.
121. Ibid, p.488.
122. Van Slambrouck, P., "Juvenile Justice: A Century of Lessons," *Christian Science Monitor*, June 29, 1999.
123. McNamee, G.H., "Introduction: 'Who is the Criminal – the State or the Child?'," in McNamee, G.H. (Ed.) *A Noble Experiment: The First 100 Years of the Cook County Juvenile Court 1899-1999* (Chicago, IL: Chicago Bar Association and Children's Court Centennial Committee, 1999), p.8.
124. Kresnak, J., "Juvenile Court Turns 100, But Is the Party Over?," *Youth Today*, vol.8, no.3, March 1999.
125. *Second Chances: 100 Years of the Children's Court* (Washington, DC: Justice Policy Institute, 1999), p.3.
126. Humes, E., *No Matter How Loud I Shout: A Year in the Life of Juvenile Court* (New York: Touchstone, 1996), pp.325-326.
127. Ayers, W., *A Kind and Just Parent: The Children of Juvenile Court* (Boston, MA: Beacon Press, 1997), p.xvi.
128. Krisberg, B., & Austin, J.F., *Reinventing Juvenile Justice* (Newbury Park, CA: Sage Publications, 1993), p.1.
129. Ayers, *A Kind and Just Parent*, supra, n.127, p.29.
130. Humes, supra, n.126, pp.78.
131. Cited in *Timeliness of the Juvenile Justice System (Report #99-03)* (Salt Lake City, Utah: Legislative Auditor General, State of Utah, 1999).
132. *Combating Violence and Delinquency: The National Juvenile Justice Action Plan Full Report* (Washington, DC: U.S. Department of Justice, 1996).
133. *Juvenile Offenders and Victims*, supra, n.70, pp.205,206.
134. DeComo, R., Tunis, S., Krisberg, B., & Herrera, N., *Juveniles Taken Into Custody Research Program: FY1992 Annual Report* (Washington, DC: Office of Juvenile Justice and Delinquency Prevention, 1993), cited in Jones, M.A., & Krisberg, B., *Images and Reality: Juvenile Crime, Youth Violence, and Public Policy* (San Francisco, CA: National Council on Crime and Delinquency, 1994), p.27.
135. Krisberg, B., Onek, D., Jones, M., & Schwartz, I., *Juveniles in State Custody: Prospects for Community-Based Care of Troubled Adolescents* (San Francisco, CA: National Council on Crime and Delinquency, 1993), cited in Jones & Krisberg, *Images and Reality*, ibid.

136. *Maryland Department of Juvenile Justice Recidivism Analyses: A Program By Program Review of Recidivism Measures at Major Facilities for Department of Juvenile Justice Youths* (Baltimore, MD: Maryland Department of Juvenile Justice, 1997), p.8.

137. Cited by Feld, B.C., *Bad Kids: Race and the Transformation of the Juvenile Court* (New York: Oxford University Press, 1999), p.280.

138. Hamparian, D.M., Schuster, R., Dinitz, D., & Conrad, J.P., *The Violent Few: A Study of Dangerous Juvenile Offenders* (Boston: Lexington Books, D.C. Heath & Company, 1978), p.119, cited in Miller, J.G., *Search and Destroy: African-American Males in the Criminal Justice System* (New York: Cambridge University Press, 1996), pp.120-121.

139. Rivers, J., & Trotti, T., *South Carolina Delinquent Males: An 11-Year Follow-Up Into Adult Probation and Prison* (Columbia, SC: South Carolina Department of Youth Services, 1995).

140. Altschuler, D.M., "Trends and Issues in the Adultification of Juvenile Justice," in Harris, P.M. (Ed), *Research to Results: Effective Community Corrections*, Proceedings of the 1995 and 1996 Conferences of the International Community Corrections Association (Lanham, MD: American Correctional Association, 1999), p.259.

141. Austin, J., Krisberg, B., & Steele, P., *Unlocking Juvenile Corrections: Evaluating the Massachusetts Department of Youth Services* (San Francisco, CA: National Council on Crime and Delinquency, 1991).

142. Data provided by Robert K. Kauffman, Missouri Division of Youth Services, telephone interview with the author, March 2000.

143. Gorsuch, K.R., Steward, M.D., Van Fleet, R.K., & Schwartz, I.M., "Missouri Division of Youth Services: An Experience in Delinquency Reform," in *Missouri and Hawaii: Leaders in Youth Correction Policy* (Ann Arbor, MI: Center for the Study of Youth Policy, 1992), pp.10-11.

144. Feld, *Bad Kids*, supra, n.137, p.279.

145. Cited in Rust, B., *Juvenile Jailhouse Rocked* (Baltimore, MD: Annie E. Casey Foundation, 1999), p.2.

146. Total expenditures for juvenile detention were almost $820 million nationwide in 1995, the last time they were calculated. Between 1995 and 1997, the detention population grew by an additional three percent.

147. Data provided by Mr. Alan Hewitt, Program Director, Juvenile Justice Center of Philadelphia, April 2000.

148. Data provided by the Philadelphia Department of Human Services.

149. Data provided by the Cook County Juvenile Probation and Court Services Department.

150. Williams, J.A., *San Francisco Juvenile Probation Department 1997 and 1998 Annual Report* (San Francisco, CA: City and County of San Francisco, 1999), and Williams, Jesse A., Chief Probation Officer of City and County of San Francisco, California, personal correspondence to the author, May 24, 2000.

151. *Guide for Implementing*, supra, n.10.

152. *Juvenile Justice: Views From Both Sides of the Aisle* (San Francisco, CA: National Council on Crime and Delinquency, 1996).

153. *A Safer Maryland: A Balanced and Restorative Juvenile Justice System – Three Year Plan 2000-2002* (Baltimore, MD: Maryland Department of Juvenile Justice, 1999), pp.18-19.

154. Joy, E.L., Testimony Before the Subcommittee on Crime of the Committee on the Judiciary, U.S. House of Representatives, March 20, 1997.

155. "State/Local Juvenile Corrections in California — A Systems Perspective," California Youth Authority, January 11, 1994, cited in *The Juvenile Crime Challenge: Making Prevention a Priority* (Sacramento, CA: Little Hoover Commission, 1994).

156. Data provided by Mr. Keller Strother, Director of MST Services, Inc., January 2000.

157. Data provided by Dr. Thomas Sexton, University of Nevada at Las Vegas, Director of Clinical Training and Practice Research Network for FFT, Inc., March 2000.

158. Richisson, T., "We don't have any place to put them," *Baltimore Sun*, December 8, 1999, p.1.

159. Altschuler, "Trends and Issues in the Adultification of Juvenile Justice," supra, n.140, pp.260-261.

160. *Promising Approaches for Graduated Sanctions* (Oakland, CA: National Council on Crime and Delinquency, n.d.), p.20.

161. Ibid.

162. Ibid.

163. *Blueprints for Violence Prevention Book Six: Multisystemic Therapy*, supra, n.1, p.xi.

164. *National Comparisons from State Recidivism Studies* (Tallahassee, FL: Florida Department of Juvenile Justice, 1999).

165. "National Status of OJJDP Prevention Program Evaluation," *Bureau of Data and Research Digest* (Tallahassee, FL: Florida Department of Juvenile Justice, 1998).

166. *Juvenile Out-of-Home Placement: A Program Evaluation Report* (St. Paul, MN: Office of the Legislative Auditor, 1999).

167. *Blueprints for Violence Prevention Book Six: Multisystemic Therapy*, supra, n.1, p.xi.

168. Zaehringer, B., *Juvenile Boot Camps: Cost and Effectiveness vs. Residential Facilities* (Topeka, KS: Koch Crime Institute, 1998), p.6.

169. Lipsey, M.W., "Juvenile Delinquency Treatment: A Meta-Analytic Inquiry Into the Variability of Effects," in Cook, T.D. et al. (Eds.), *Meta-Analysis for Explanation: A Casebook* (New York: Russell Sage Foundation, 1992), cited in Howell, supra, n.10, p.138.

170. Gottfredson, D.C., "School-Based Crime Prevention," in Sherman, L., Gottfredson, D., MacKenzie, D., Eck, J., Reuter, P., & Bushway, S., *Preventing Crime: What Works, What Doesn't, What's Promising*, Report to the United States Congress (Washington, DC: National Institute of Justice, 1997).

171. Brooks, Schiraldi,& Ziedenberg, supra, n.69, pp.16-17.

172. Ibid, p.24.

173. Ibid, p.24.

174. Data retrieved from *Office of Juvenile Justice Statistical Briefing Book*, online, at http://www.ojjdp.ncjrs.org/ojstatbb/JuvenileArrestRates.html.

175. Data retrieved from *Office of Juvenile Justice Statistical Briefing Book*, online, at http://www.ojjdp.ncjrs.org/ojstatbb/qa179.html.

176. Altschuler, D.M., "Issues and Challenges in the Community Supervision of Juvenile Offenders," *Southern Illinois University Law Journal*, vol.23, Winter 1999, pp.2-3.

177. Miller, *Search and Destroy*, supra, n.138, p.113.

178. *Juvenile Offenders and Victims*, supra, n.70, p.192.

179. Data reported in Schiraldi, V., testimony before the Committee on Education and the Workforce's Subcommittee on Early Childhood, Youth, and Families, March 18, 1999 .

180. Pope, C., & Feyerherm, W., *Minorities and the Juvenile Justice System: Final Report* (Washington, DC: Office of Juvenile Justice and Delinquency Prevention, 1991), cited in *Juvenile Offenders and Victims: 1999 National Report*, supra, n.70, p.193.

181. *Juvenile Offenders and Victims*, supra, n.70, p.182.

182. Feld, *Bad Kids*, supra, n137, p.125.

183. Parent, D.G., Leiter, V., Kennedy, S., Livens, L., Wentworth, D., & Wilcox, S., *Conditions of Confinement: A Study to Evaluate Conditions in Juvenile Detention and Corrections Facilities - Executive Summary* (Washington, DC: Office of Juvenile Justice and Delinquency Prevention, 1993).

184. Hargrove, M., "Welcome to Hell," *Arkansas Democrat-Gazette*, June 14, 1998, p.1.

185. Butterfield, F., "Hard Time: A Special Report.; Profits at a Juvenile Prison Come With a Chilling Cost," *New York Times*, July 15, 1998, p.1.

186. *Juvenile Detention and Training School Crowding: A Clearinghouse of Court Cases* (Richmond, KY: National Juvenile Detention Association, 1998).

187. Ayers, *A Kind and Just Parent*, supra, n.127, p.40.

188. Juvenile Offender Aftercare Assessment Team, *Executive Summary of the Report to Governor Parris N. Glendening and Lt. Governor Kathleen Kennedy Townsend* (Baltimore, MD: Maryland Department of Juvenile Justice, 2000).

189. Hawkins, J.D., & Catalano, R., *Communities That Care: Risk-Focused Prevention Using the Social Development Strategy* (Seattle, WA: Developmental Research and Programs, Inc., 1993).

190. Duggan, A.K., McFarlane, E.C., Windham, A.M., Rohde, C.A., Salkever, D.S., Fuddy, L, Rosenberg, L.A., Buchbinder, S.B., Sia, C.C.J., "Evaluation of Hawaii's Healthy Start Program," *Future of Children*, vol.9, no.1, Spring/Summer 1999.

191. St. Pierre, R.G., Layzer, J.I., Goodson, B.D., & Bernstein, L.S., *The Effectiveness of Comprehensive Case Management Interventions: Findings from the National Evaluation of the Comprehensive Child Development Program* (Cambridge, MA: Abt Associates, 1997), p.6.

192. Ibid, p.16.

193 Frede, E.C., "The Role of Program Quality in Producing Early Childhood Program Benefits," *The Future of Children,* Vol. 5 . No. 3, Winter 1995.

194. Yoshikawa, H., "Long-Term Effects of Early Childhood Programs on Social Outcomes and Delinquency," *The Future of Children,* Vol. 5 . No. 3, Winter 1995.

195. *Head Start: Research Provides Little Information on Impact of Current Program*, Letter Report GAO/HEHS_97_59 (Washington, DC: General Accounting Office, 1997).

196. Lawrence Sherman, Testimony Before the Subcommittee on Crime, U.S. House of Representatives Committee on the Judiciary, October 28, 1999.

197. Rosenbaum, D.P., & Hanson, G.S., "Assessing the Effects of School-Based Drug Education" A Six-Year Multi-Level Analysis of Project D.A.R.E.," *Journal of Research in Crime and Delinquency*, vol.35, no.4, November 1998, pp.381-412.

198. Gottfredson, D.C., "School-Based Crime Prevention," supra, n.170.

199. Silvia, E.S., Thorne, J., & Tashjian, C. (1997). *School-Based Drug Prevention Programs: A Longitudinal Study in Selected School Districts. Final Report*. Washington, DC: U.S. Department of Education, p.25, and Modzeleski, W., Testimony Before the Committee on Health, Education, Labor, and Pensions of the U.S. Senate, July 13, 1999.

200. Silvia et al, ibid, p.24.

201. Ibid, p.23.

202. Ibid, p.22

203. Ibid, p.28.

204. *What is Known About the Link Between Child Maltreatment and Delinquency?*, unpublished fact sheet provided by the Child Welfare League of America, March 2000.

205. *Issue Briefing: DSS Gateway to Juvenile Crime* (Boston, MA: Citizens for Juvenile Justice, January 2000).

206. Geen, R., & Tumlin, K.C., *State Efforts to Remake Child Welfare: Responses to New Challenges and Increased Security* (Washington, DC: Urban Institute, 1999), pp.4-6.

207. Dissemination information provided by Dr. Carolyn Webster-Stratton, May 2000.

208. Bilchik, S., *Mental Health Disorders and Substance Abuse Problems Among Juveniles* (Washington, DC: Office of Juvenile Justice and Delinquency Prevention, July 1998).

209. *Mental Health: A Report of the Surgeon General*, supra, n.24.

210. Ibid.

211. Cited in *Mental Health: A Report from the Surgeon General*, ibid.

212. Dr, Thomas Sexton, telephone interview with the author, March 2000.

213. Melton, G.B., "Why Don't the Knuckleheads Use Common Sense?," in Henggeler, S.W., & Santos, A.B. (Eds.), *Innovative Approaches for Difficult-to-Treat Populations* (Washington, DC: American Psychiatric Press, 1997), p.354.

214. Latessa, E.J., Moon, M. M., & Applegate, B.K., *Preliminary Evaluation of the Ohio Department of Youth Services Reclaim Ohio Project: Executive Summary* (Cincinnati, OH: (University of Cincinnati Division of Criminal Justice, 1995), and Moon, M. M., Applegate, B.K., & Latessa, E.J., "Reclaim Ohio: A Politically Viable Alternative to Treating Youthful Felony Offenders," *Crime and Delinquency*, vol. 43, no.4, October 1997, pp.438-456.

215. *Analysis of the 1999-00 Budget Bill* (Sacramento, CA: Legislative Analyst's Office, 1999), p.D-100.

216. Wilson, J.Q., "What If Anything Can the Federal Government Do About Crime?," seminar presentation at the National Institute of Justice "Perspectives on Crime and Justice" series, December 10, 1996, cited in *Briefing Sheet: Federalization of Juvenile Crime* (Washington, DC: Center for An Effective Crime Policy, 1998).

217. *Program Accountability Measures for DJJ Commitment Programs: A Two-Year Analysis FY 1999-2000* (Tallahassee, FL: Florida Department of Juvenile Justice, 2000).

218. *Juvenile Justice: Status of Delinquency Prevention Program and Description of Local Projects*, Letter Report GAO/GGD96147 (Washington, DC: General Accounting Office, 1996).

APPENDIX I

Reducing Juvenile Crime: Recommendations from America's Police Chiefs

1) Which of these Strategies do Police Chiefs Believe are the Most Effective for Reducing Juvenile Crime?

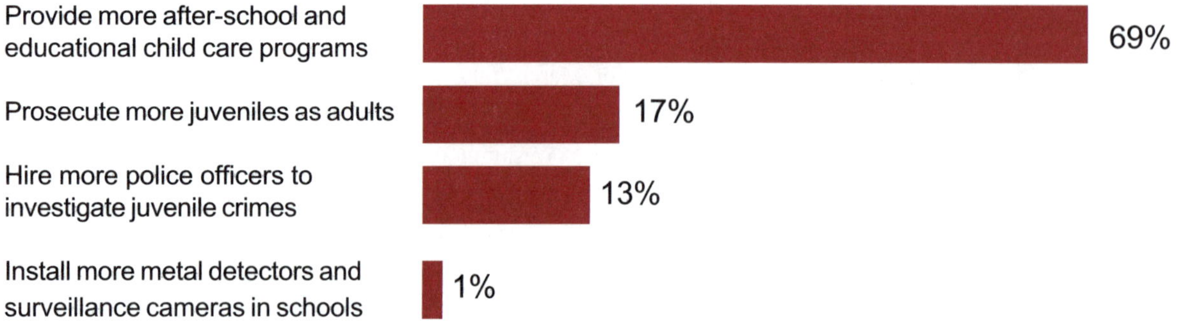

Percentages shown above are those ranked "1" by Police Chiefs on a scale of 1 to 4.

2) The Police Chiefs were asked "Please rate the following strategies on a scale of 1 to 5 on their value as a crime prevention tool." This chart shows the percentage for each strategy that received a "1" rating by the Police Chiefs.

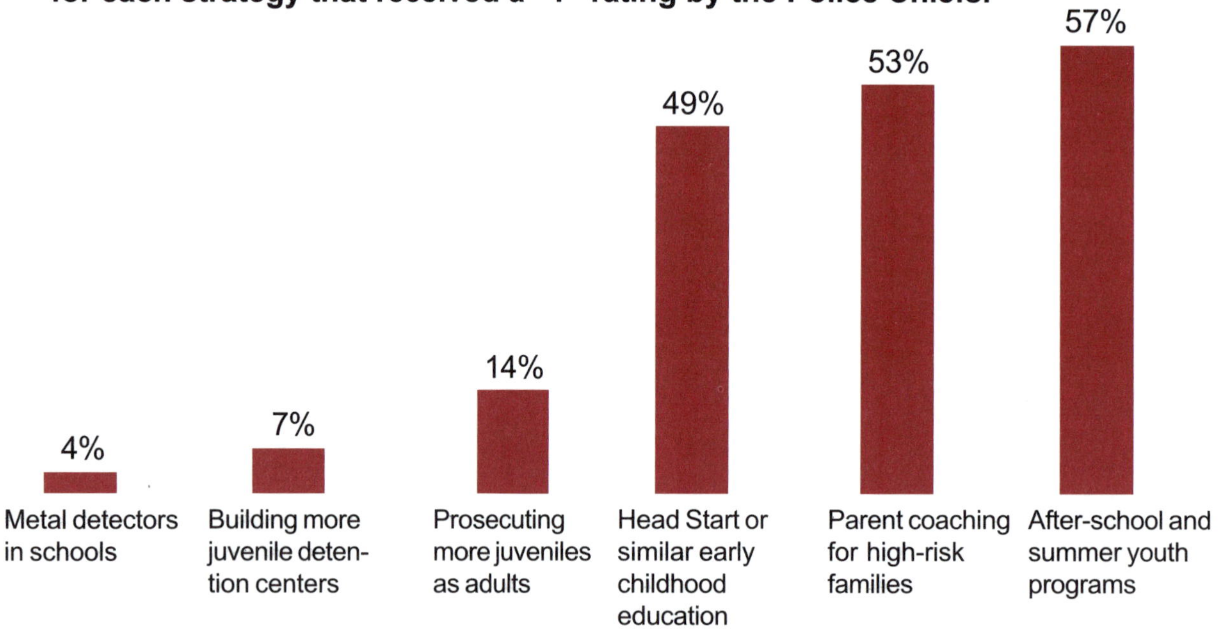

The poll was conducted for *Fight Crime: Invest in Kids*, from October 14th through the 27th, 1999. 855 Chiefs were surveyed, from a sample including all 255 Chiefs from cities over 100,000, and a random sample of 600 Chiefs serving smaller cities. 566 Chiefs responded to the survey (66%), and the margin of error was 5%.

Source: Mashtrofski, S., and S. Keeter, *Poll of Police Chiefs,* online at: http://www.fightcrime.org/pdf/police_chiefs_poll_report.pdf.

APPENDIX II

The Costs of Juvenile Crime

In 1998, Vanderbilt University economist Mark A. Cohen calculated the cost to American taxpayers when a young person drops out of high school to embrace a life of crime and drugs. Based on Cohen's analysis, the National Center for Juvenile Justice prepared the following "invoice":

INVOICE

To: American Public
For: One Lost Youth

DESCRIPTION	COST
Crime:	
Juvenile Career (4 years @ 1-4 crimes/year)	
Victim Costs	$62,000 - $250,000
Criminal Justice Costs	$21,000 - $84,000
Adult Career (6 years @ 10.6 crimes/year)	
Victim Costs	$1,000,000
Criminal Justice Costs	$335,000
Offender Productivity Loss	$64,000
Total Crime Cost	**$1.5 - $1.8 million**
Present Value*	**$1.3 - $1.5 million**
Drug Abuse:	
Resources Devoted to Drug Market	$84,000 - $168,000
Reduced Productivity Loss	$27,600
Drug Treatment Costs	$10,200
Medical Treatment of Drug Related Illness	$11,000
Premature Death	$31,800 - $223,000
Criminal Justice Costs associated with Drug Crimes	$40,500
Total Drug Abuse Costs	**$200,000 - $480,000**
Present Value*	**$150,000 - $360,000**
Costs Imposed by High School Dropout:	
Lost Wage Productivity	$300,000
Fringe Benefits	$75,000
Nonmarket Losses	$95,000 - $375,000
Total Dropout Cost	**$470,000 - $750,000**
Present Value*	**$243,000 - $388,000**
Total Loss	**$2.2 - $3 million**
Present Value*	**$1.7 - $2.3 million**

*Present Value is the amount of money that would have to be invested **today** in order to cover future costs of the youth's behavior.

Source: National Center for Juvenile Justice, an adaptation of Cohen's "The Monetary Value of Saving a High-Risk Youth," Journal of Quantitative Criminology, 14(1), reprinted from Juvenile Offenders and Victims: 1999 National Report (Pittsburgh, PA: National Center for Juvenile Justice, 1999), p.82.

Invoice available at: http://www.ncjrs.org/html/ojjdp/nationalreport99/chapter3.pdf